The Bear-Proof Investor

JOHN F. WASIK

The Bear-Proof

Investor

Prospering Safely in Any Market

An Owl Book

Henry Holt and Company • New York

Henry Holt and Company, LLC
Publishers since 1866
115 West 18th Street
New York, New York 10011

Henry Holt® is a registered trademark of
Henry Holt and Company, LLC.

Distributed in Canada by H. B. Fenn and Company Ltd.

Library of Congress Cataloging-in-Publication Data

Wasik, John F.
The bear-proof investor : prospering safely in any market / John F. Wasik.—1st ed.
p. cm.
"An owl book."
Includes bibliographical references and index.
ISBN: 0-8050-7019-2 (pbk.)
1. Investments. I. Title.

HG4521 .W245 2002
332.63'2—dc21   2002017220

Henry Holt books are available for special promotions and
premiums. For details contact: Director, Special Markets.

First Edition 2002
Printed in the United States of America

1 3 5 7 9 10 8 6 4 2

For Julia Theresa

Contents

Acknowledgments

This book would not be possible without the gracious assistance and support of many investment professionals, friends, colleagues, and loved ones.

First of all, my heart belongs to my three leading ladies—Kathleen Rose, Sarah Virginia, and Julia Theresa—whose intelligence, patience, beauty, and love are the best support an author could ever hope for in the best and worst of times.

My agent and friend Robert Shepard and my editors John Sterling, David Sobel, Robin Dennis, and everyone at Henry Holt and Company made this project come alive. And kudos to my Holt publicist Jenny Chikes.

Special thanks to the great money managers who gave generously of their time and talent, particularly Chris Brown, Bill Miller, John Rogers, Clyde McGregor, Leah Zell, Sam Isaly, Carlton Martin, and George Fisher. It's not easy to snag some quality time with leading mutual fund managers, especially when they are doing well managing billions of dollars of other people's money—and trying not to lose it in a down market.

It would not be possible to feature these fine investment minds without the support and coordination of the people behind them, namely, Mary Ann Murphy of Pax; Meg Pier of Eaton Vance; Kelli Arnold of Oakmark; Merrilyn Kosier and Mellody Hobson of Ariel; Charlene Petzing of Liberty-Acorn, Audrey Conley and Moira Fox of Legg Mason; and Tom Pinto and Pat O'Connor of TIAA-CREF.

I have a special thank you reserved for my favorite reference librarians at the Grayslake, Illinois, Public Library, whom I have tortured with requests for obscure investment texts over several months' time, and Ellen Bull of the Society of Actuaries, who granted me access to their special library (even though I wasn't a member).

A special word of recognition goes to my colleagues at *Consumers Digest* magazine. Although we all lost our once-secure jobs partially due to the dot.com madness, it was great sharing some ego space, torments, and laughs for the past fifteen years or so.

Most of all, I'd like to dedicate this book to the thousands who lost their lives on September 11. Far too many of them were in the financial services businesses that I've been writing about for the past twenty years. Their memory is our purpose.

Preface

In my modest existence on this earth, I've lived through three wars, a half-dozen bear markets, and one bona fide stock market crash. Although I was too young to remember, I also lived through the Cuban Missile Crisis, in which our country was on the brink of war. President Kennedy was considering limited nuclear strikes on the Soviet Union, which seems, in retrospect, to dwarf all of our current crises when you give it some careful thought. And then there were the assassinations of President Kennedy, his brother Bobby, Martin Luther King, and the tumult that followed. I distinctly remember the look of fear in my father's eyes—something I had never seen before—when he talked about how the conflagration on the West Side of Chicago following Dr. King's murder might come down to our little hamlet south of the city. This social unrest would later find its way into my high school, where there was a minor race riot my freshman year. I can remember the doors of the washrooms being locked to prevent random beatings in my integrated school. At that time, the fear was in *my* eyes.

In our current time of crisis and conflict, our society is being violently propelled into a future with scintillating new challenges. There is this disequilibrium about, and every institution from the stock exchanges to the White House is trying to balance the scales again. It is as if some plague of locusts has descended upon our verdant, open fields of endless growth and ravaged our society—for the time being. The ecology of this situation is that our civilization *will* balance the disharmonies. On a personal level, though, what do we do? We have bills to pay, retirements to fund, houses to repair, and children to educate.

We still have a need to finance these items, the bountiful garden of our future. As the markets, governments, and armies work to right the balances in the external world, we need to find balance in our own life, a *personal* ecology that provides bread on our table and the sustenance for the days ahead. So we start by understanding our own needs, the material demands of living a life of our own free choosing.

There will always be bear markets. Excesses in capitalism will be rectified the way a forest or prairie is eventually returned to health after a fire. We will recover and prosper. We always have. There also will be opportunities to find the right investments for our short-term needs (over the next five years) and beyond. For example, the industrialized world is aging, benefiting from technology, and still relatively prosperous. Opportunities that spring from these facts of life are abundant, even in the worst of economic climates. Companies that make food, drugs, digital switches, medical devices, and biotechnology and that provide services to manage money will still be in business for decades to come. They are like Hermes, messengers of a new, healthier age, symbols of a material future filled with hope and promise of a new prosperity.

The Western world has been through crisis before, however, and survived. Feudalism, imperialism, fascism, communism—all were vanquished. Social and economic systems after these cataclysms were restructured and made stronger. World War II alone ended with an economic pact that aided all of Western Europe, Japan, and China. Now it may be the Third World's turn for bolstering, a recognition that we need to enter the narrow gate of global charity and understanding.

We are obliged to remember that British economist John Maynard Keynes said that the Great Depression was about the failure of a discouraged people to take a risk. My contention is that if we understand risk, we have a fresh perspective on our lives, and failure becomes a keystone to learning. And an enlightened approach to risk over time makes us prosperous.

By showing you the ways of approaching risk in your investments, you will be able to stay focused and take a rational path. Whether it's secure retirement or funding some short-term goals, *The Bear-Proof Investor* is my view on not eliminating risk or avoiding down markets, but knowing how to regard adversity as an opportunity and bravely embrace the future with hope and an eye on a sustainable prosperity.

Introduction

It was a time when space mattered. Not outer space, which is becoming increasingly harder to see with the naked eye due to all of the light pollution. Not the inner space of cells, molecules, and atoms, which is becoming increasingly probed and manipulated to tinker with nature's operating code. I'm referring to a time of *ego* space, the great abstract expanse of the self, when the center of the universe became the material self and that was all that mattered. This era of the ever-expanding ego space manifested itself in a number of ways.

Expanded ego space meant bigger everything. New homes were enlarged with huge atriums, bathrooms, living rooms, and bedrooms that had high ceilings and mostly air. Vehicles got bigger. Most of the leviathans were really pickup trucks with leather reclining seats that ate gasoline the way a football lineman bulks up for the big game. These trucks, however, were sold and priced like luxury sedans. Inebriated with power and space, these behemoths mostly lumbered to the shopping malls, soccer fields, and supermarkets and back, all of which also grew and expanded in the age of the ego.

Then there was the human body itself, the vessel of the fragile, ever-unsatisfied ego. Bolstered by an endless variety of supplements, diets, personal trainers, exercise machines, implants, Prozac, and Viagra, the body also expanded in ways never thought possible. Life spans increased and scientists were talking about 130-year life spans as being likely, if not probable.

Powered by information and technology, the ego space continuum shot forth on fiber tendrils of glass across the globe in cyberspace. Everyone could have ego space accessible by anyone else in cyberspace with a computer, modem, and phone line. Web sites, the abstract graphic symbol of ego, flourished. As a result, commerce, the ego-savants promised, would be forever faster and cheaper to transact because everyone could have a virtual business in their own home from their own computer. Whole warehouses and distribution networks would be replaced with the silvery tendrils and laptop terminals.

The stock market, in turn, responded by creating huge wealth, the dowry of the marriage between ego- and cyberspace. This money bought even bigger houses, cars, boats, and bodies. Some ego-space billionaires bought other bodies as surrogate armies of strength and virility (in the form of professional athletes). When they tired of their boats, airplanes, and real estate, the most powerful ego-space magnates started giving their money away to worthy causes, to justify the universal beneficence of their self-worth.

Like Icarus thinking he could fly to the sun on wax wings, however, the ego space collapsed on itself. Like an algae bloom, the growth of investment capital, infrastructure, and ego space crashed when demand (the food supply that drives capitalism) and the realities of profit-making were revealed to be part of the fractured mythology of ego space. The gods had descended from Mount Olympus to battle the titans of an imbalanced market and restore order.

There were no innocent bystanders when ego space was sucked into the gravity of the black hole of economic reality. We all had egos that rose with the stock market indices. Some egos truly were obsessed with the idea that this economy was *new*, it was *different*. *It* didn't follow the rules that have governed markets for hundreds of years. After all, *this* technology was *creating* jobs, moving information at lower cost, restructuring capitalism itself. Those who had a piece of this new railroad of growth would be wealthy without having to work for it.

In our ego age, the dot.coms turned into *dot.cons*. The brilliant Icaruses who got billions of other people's ego money to start up their winged ventures were suddenly out of money and out of work. Even the once-mighty vestiges of the old economy who dipped their feet in the River Styx to seek telecosmic immortality—the AT&Ts, Cornings, and Lucents—melted when the sun of profit reality shone on them. When it all came down to earth, the ego space was worth about $3 trillion less than when the great ego pump-up began. Wealth begotten by the promise of information technology creating untold trillions simply melted with each passing day. It was your 401(k) money, your brother-in-law's Cisco stock, my wife's SEP-IRA, my retirement nest egg.

Our Time Is No Different
from Previous Booms and Busts

Despite my psychohistory of the past twenty years, what has happened to us also describes the 1870s, 1890s, early 1900s, 1920s, 1950s, 1960s, and 1983 to the present. Every explosion of technology (or end of a war) is immediately followed by a boom in the financial markets. The technology then becomes commonplace and commodity-like, when the value of it crashes until the next wave comes along. Railroads and land speculation blossomed following the Civil War, until there were too many railroads; then they started to go bankrupt. The telegraph created another minitechnology boom, followed by the many inventions of Edison and the electrification of cities and factories. The early part of the century saw the emergence of the internal combustion engine, which became possible after the invention of efficient means of exploring, distributing, and refining petroleum. And so on into our present age of genomics, nanotechnology, and supercomputing.

Each generation has seen this unique combination of demographic and technological uplift, excess, and equilibrium. It's chaos theory writ large in history. Not only was the technology that was invented in each era expanding opportunities and creating wealth, each contemporary generation was always young enough and open-minded enough to appreciate it—and consume the new wave of goods and services. It's like the growth of mushrooms, which only sprout up after sufficient quantities of rain, detritus, and sunlight provide the right balance for growth.

During the expansion of technology, the ever-inflating ego space negates the rules of prudent investing for an ever-brief period of euphoria. We are hooked on the materialistic endorphins that make us believe that the growth is endless, the wealth permanent, the gains a way of life. Instead of making safe bets on the entire universe of stocks, bonds, and real estate, we concentrated our holdings on the twenty to one hundred most glorious companies Wall Street ever created. We paid dearly for our vanity and greed, like so many others before us investing in instant cameras, railroads, land speculation, and tulips. Even the wise and witty Mark Twain was constantly getting burned on investing in new inventions that were "the next best thing."

There are natural laws that govern markets and economies, although those laws are subject to many permutations because ego space is constantly warping due to its curved and unpredictable nature. In years past, the fave raves were the Beatles, 'N Sync, and Beanie Baby dolls. Tomorrow it will be designer human beings. There are no straight lines in ego space.

Some laws, however, remain fairly constant and they concern risk, return, and how to measure these intangible guidelines of how to invest. Many of these rules follow the science of ecology, where balance and relationships need to be understood before you proceed into the world of stocks and bonds. For my purposes here, ecology is a personal study of how we connect with our material world—a *personal* ecology—that will help us understand how to create wealth sustainably without destroying our life savings.

How You Can Use This Book

I'll not only revisit the immutable rules of risk and return, I'll illustrate how they can work for you so that you can create a balanced, risk-adjusted portfolio that will survive the unknowable and unpredictable void of ego space. Although I don't know if there is truly such as thing as a "bear-proof investor"—you can get burned even if you put all of your money in your mattress (inflation will rob you of purchasing power)—I'll teach you how to create a bear-proof portfolio that will survive the ravages of ego space and uncertain markets. It may surprise you that I have no novel techniques for beating the market in bad times. This book isn't about speculation, options, or technical strategies that few can practice. It's about a consistent method of investing that, over time, is likely to reap enough returns to beat inflation and allow you to meet all of your investment goals.

Even if you got through the last few years unscathed, I believe you'll benefit from the timeless insights from some of the world's wisest investors and their philosophies of balance and purpose, which I've profiled. After all, before you can invest sensibly and safely, you need to have a sound personal ecology, a balance between your needs, the rational laws of the market, and the natural unpredictability of human beings moving that market.

This is a journey starting with my own humble tale. You'll meet some remarkable people who know their craft better than anyone. I'll tell you how they work and how they survive nasty markets with proven strategies that you can use. More important, we'll have some fun using their principles to build your own bear-proof portfolio.

I've written this book as an intermediate yet fundamental approach to investing. I'm assuming you've been investing for years through your company pension plan, 401(k), 403(b), Keogh, SEP-IRA, or SIMPLE. If, for some reason, you haven't set up a retirement plan or haven't saved a dime, I'd like to refer you to my *Late-Start Investor* (Owl, 1999) or *Kitchen-Table Investor* (Owl, 2001). These books give you the fundamentals on how to save and set up retirement plans. For those relatively close to retirement, more advanced information on retirement planning is contained in my *Retire Early—and Live the Life You Want Now* (Owl, 2001).

I will show you how some of the best financial minds select their investments and give you an overview of their methods. I will bring you into their worlds and highlight their triumphs and discuss their weaknesses. Better yet, I'll offer you the best of class in a range of investment styles. Along the way, I'll discuss the importance of long-term investing in stocks, bonds, cash, real estate, and mutual funds of all stripes. If you don't have the least interest in how all this works, simply dart to chapter 11, where I provide bearproof portfolios for nearly every type of investor. Moreover, I'll even discuss some of the instructive mistakes *I've* made over the years and how you can employ the most tried-and-true ways of successful investing to prosper in any market.

I'm also assuming that you've been through the last few years of the stock market and suffered some bumps and bruises. And like me, you've probably lost some money and are seeking the middle road between the stratospheric highs and catastrophic lows of investing for total return.

Whether you have primarily invested through mutual funds (in and out of your employer's plan) or through individual stocks and bonds, I'll show you some risk-averse techniques that have been proven winners over time. Whether you prefer the professional management of mutual funds or want to buy stocks on your own, there are pearls for every type of investor.

CHAPTER 1

Dancing Bubble Bears:
A Brief History of Bear Markets,
Booms, Busts, Risk, and What to Expect

*Prosperity is not without many fears and distastes; and adversity
is not without comforts and hopes. . . . Certainly virtue is like
previous odors, most fragrant when they are incensed, or crushed;
for prosperity doth best discover vice, but adversity doth best discover virtue.*

—Francis Bacon

The bubble bear danced in my head more than once over the past
few years. Its growl, however, sounded like celestial music when
the market soared, making me giddy with the thought of making
more money in the stock market than working for an employer.
She was wearing a tutu, dancing on floating bubbles, light as a
cloud, soaring up higher and higher until . . . reality hit about two
years ago. My 401(k) account balance fell precipitously. Instead of
making $1,000 a day, I was losing $2,000 a day. My wife's SEP-
IRA accounts—all in technology and sector funds—didn't drop as
much, but they made her sick with anxiety.

"Stay the course," the bear in the pink tights sang to me. And I
did. Stayed in the high flyers whose upside at one time knew no
bounds. She was a bear in my dreams, but she was a *ballerina*,
pirouetting with each new market high. In my subconscious, I
never questioned why she was a bear and not a bull, but dreams

always speak truth in the form of images, if not borderline hallucinations.

Stock-market investing in the late 1990s was a hypnotic dream from which we've only begun to regain consciousness. Like the mythical dancing bear, it rarely stumbled, but mostly ascended on a bubble; it was the cherub of the new economy because *everything* had changed. It had to go up, it was the granite base of the info economy. What was the downside if *everyone* was investing in info technology at the same time? Could millions of investors and trillions of dollars be wrong?

I lost $30,000 on paper before I bailed out of my high-technology funds. Further market declines eroded my wealth by another $30,000. My wife lost the $10,000 she contributed to her SEP-IRAs before we "reallocated" into more conservative mutual funds (see chapter 11). That was how I stopped thinking about the dancing bubble bear. I no longer felt wealthy. The ballet was over. It was time for lower-risk investments, something safe and sustainable. And so the story begins of how I learned to ignore the dancing bubble bear and get on with my life.

Why You'll Have Some Fun

Although my family and I came out just fine in the dot.com crash—better than ever, in fact—I had a great time tracking down some of the most durable investment strategies of all time. Some of the techniques are familiar to anyone who's dabbled in investing. Others are not so familiar and deserve a closer look. In any case, this book is an exploration of ideas and philosophies of investing based on my idea that you need a sound "personal ecology" in your life, meaning a harmonious balance among the different facets of daily living (work, family, community, spiritual, and material needs).

My investing philosophy, however, goes beyond this short list of life tasks. We need to know when we are out of balance with all of the parts that make up our whole. In an ecological sense, if there are too many predators and not enough prey in an ecosystem, then there's starvation or migration.

The same principle applies to our money lives. If we are placing all of our bets on a small part of the stock market, we are taking undue risks that throw our entire material life out of balance. With the ideas I'll be discussing, you can reexamine your whole portfolio with an eye on risk while gaining sustainable returns.

All of the fine money managers I've interviewed have an impeccable sense of balance. They know where they need to be and where they shouldn't. That isn't to say they haven't made mistakes or had bad years in which very little they tried worked. Although they all need to make educated guesses about where they think the market may be headed, they don't try to predict the market in the short term. They spread their money out among hundreds of securities to blunt the effect of being in the wrong place at the wrong time. By *diversifying* among a broad variety of securities, they lower their overall risk, or the possibility that their securities will suddenly drop in value. The best managers are buying quality stocks, bonds, and real estate when others are selling. In this way, they are true investors, putting their faith in the market's ability to realize the true value of an investment over time. This is a perfect principle for any investor, no matter how sophisticated.

Discovering that it's relatively easy to create a portfolio that is adjusted for risk is the most satisfying part of what I am about to reveal. It works for anybody and you don't need to have an Ivy League degree to appreciate how it will enrich you. It can also be fun, when you realize that you can make money in down markets when others are losing their shirts.

Back to the Bear and Bubbles: Some History

So where did this $3 trillion go that went scurrying away in the night? Why did 401(k) assets drop an average $4,821 in 2000, the first decline in twenty years after a decade of unprecedented growth?

It is the nature of bubbles and bears—especially those that involve dancing—that few participants know what is happening until the bubbles burst. The dot.com blowout is really nothing new. Other bubbles have burst and people have survived them. The following are a few notable bubbles from the past that are worth revisiting:

- Tulip Mania. The normally astute and commercially minded Dutch launched a fever called "tulip mania" in 1634 in the time of Rembrandt. Charles MacKay detailed the craze in his 1841 classic *Extraordinary Popular Delusions and the Madness of Crowds*, which is still in print. Tulip bulbs were the rage and investors were willing to pay almost any price for them. Some of the bulbs were rare; some were not. A speculative hysteria took hold. As MacKay recounts: "People of all professions turned their property into cash; houses and furniture were offered at ruinous prices; the idea spread throughout the country that the passion for tulips would last forever; and when it was known that foreigners were seized with the fever, it was believed that the wealth of the world would concentrate on the shores of the *Zuider Zee*, and that poverty would become a memory in Holland." Like those who bet on Cisco and Lucent going up forever, this fad came down hard and fast.

- The Mississippi Scheme. A self-styled Scottish "economist" by the name of John Law talked the French court and thousands of French investors into investing in a bank that supported trading companies in then-untested frontier colonies of Louisiana and Mississippi. A handsome gambler and murderer, "Beau" Law eventually gained the support of Louis XIV, who was swimming in debt from wars and his own profligate living. In 1718, Law's scheme was declared a royal bank by the king and operated under the protection of the Duc d'Orléans, the regent of France. This decree caused the stock in the bank to rise twentyfold, so that by 1719 the bank was worth more than eighty times all of the currency in France. A shortage of shares then created a speculative frenzy. French bankers decided that they could pay off the national debt of France with shares from Law's company. The only problem was that Law's scheme was backed by false credit and the whole affair came tumbling down, plunging the government into bankruptcy and ruining tens of thousands of families. Law barely escaped with his life, eventually dying in poverty in Venice in 1729 and insisting on his deathbed that his bank was sound.

- The South Sea Bubble. This British trading company had a monopoly over the new trade routes to the South Seas in 1720. Shares of the company were trading wildly in London's "Exchange Alley," climbing as much as 1,000 percent. Someone asked Sir Isaac Newton how high the shares could climb and he retorted, "I cannot calculate the madness of the people." The shares finally crashed.

- The "New Technologies." Can you name a dozen railroads, steel companies, telegraph operations, and teletype concerns? Remember the New York Central or Western Union? How about linotype manufacturers (the hot type used by newspapers before lithography and computerized typesetting), Hollerith adding machines, and steam-powered factories? All attracted the speculative dollars of investors over the last 150 years or so. Take a look at the following list of companies that were the top companies in terms of stock-market capitalization (share price times outstanding shares) in 1912 at the height of the first information revolution, when electric appliances, lighting, telephones, and automobiles thrust the world into the modern age:

SURVIVORS AND SO-LONGS: TOP COMPANIES OF 1912

Company	Market Value ($ in Billions)
U.S. Steel	$0.74
Standard Oil	$0.39
J&P Coates	$0.29
Pullman	$0.20
Royal Dutch	$0.19
Anaconda	$0.18
General Electric	$0.17
Singer	$0.17
American Brands	$0.17
International Harvester	$0.16

TOP CORPORATIONS OF OUR TIME

Company	Market Value ($ in Billions)
General Electric	$409
Microsoft	$301
Exxon Mobil	$284
Pfizer	$259
Wal-Mart	$229
Citigroup	$218
Royal Dutch/Shell	$196
Vodaphone	$189
NTT DoCoMo	$189
BP Amoco	$188

Exxon Mobil was partially formed from two companies from the Standard Oil breakup early in the century. International Harvester shed its agricultural-implement and construction businesses and became Navistar, a truck manufacturer. General Electric has added hundreds of businesses since Thomas Edison founded it largely to manufacture electrical-generating and distribution equipment. Market caps as of 4/01. *Source: The Economist.*

As you can see, capitalism is an ever-dynamic force that is shaped by markets, consumer demand, economies of scale, and technology. As humans with brains that run on emotions as well as reason, we get caught up in the latest technological revolution. Think of how the world was captivated by mass installations of electric lighting. Our days became infinite inside our own homes. Or when we could call across the ocean at the speed of light or make the kind of structural steel that could support a hundred-story building. Who would not be moved by these great accomplishments the way we are awed by stem-cell research, computers that fit on your wrist, and drugs that cure nearly every infectious disease?

Although much of this may sound familiar—and the consumer/business press has regurgitated this history of manias many times by now—investors generally have short memories. We still are motivated by broker and brother-in-law tips or "somebody who works for the company." And this mentality has been in place as long as anyone can remember. We did not outgrow investing by rumor over the last several years as we progressed from the age of "Greed Is Good" to "Where's Mine?"* Not that I find anything wrong with making money when the market is moving up. You'd be a fool not to participate (many didn't and lost ground to plain old inflation and stagnant wages). After all, you didn't have to dig ditches or clean toilets to make money in a market that couldn't lose. How do you avoid bubbles and manias when so many are convinced that it's the right thing to do? How do you avoid being slaughtered as part of the herd? You need to be realistic about long-term returns.

Being Realistic: The Age of Reduced Expectations

Despite the technology-heavy NASDAQ Index losing up to 60 percent of its value during the dot.com crash, investors remained unusually optimistic about the stock market. After all, in an age of elevated ego space, we've come to expect double-digit returns in the market. It's become an accepted fact in the information economy. So it wasn't surprising that the *Wall Street Journal* reported in a survey of investors in April 2001—after a solid year of declines—that "the average American investor still expects double-digit future annual gains . . . about one American in five, in fact, expects stock investments to gain more than 20% in a normal year."

I hate to disagree with the Bard, but when it comes to stock and bond markets, "past is *not* prologue." Just because stocks returned an average 16 percent a year for the fifteen years ending in 2000 doesn't mean that will always be the case. As historical data from Ibbotson Associates points out, if you take sixty-one rolling periods

---

*Actually this slogan was the late, great Chicago columnist Mike Royko's retranslation of the Chicago motto *Urbs in Horto*, which is Latin for "City in a Garden." Although Royko was referring to political corruption in the Windy City, another sense of entitlement applies here.

(of fifteen years each going back seventy-five years), there were just thirteen occasions when stocks generated 16 percent a year or more. Two of those periods, surprisingly, were in the late 1950s and early 1960s when most people weren't investing in the stock market en masse and mutual funds were a spark of what they are today.

Based on the unlikely scenario of double-digit returns continuing, Jonathan Clements of the *Wall Street Journal* warns, "Think you will earn 16% a year over the next 15 years? I wouldn't bank on it. For starters, you probably don't keep 100% of your portfolio in stocks and bonds."

Clements has plenty of company when it comes to predicting an era of diminished returns. Academics and industry experts who have been charting the market's progress and history their entire careers are stating their case for single-digit stock returns. Professors Eugene Fama and Kenneth French, two highly respected researchers from the University of Chicago and Massachusetts Institute of Technology, respectively, have studied stock returns over the past 130 years. The annual average stock-market return from 1972 through 1949, for example, was 8.8 percent. From 1950 through 1999, the postwar expansion boosted stock returns to the 14.8 percent annual average return. The two professors lean toward the earlier period as being the *normal* range of returns. They contend that in the expansion following World War II, investors were willing to pay a higher premium for taking more risk, not surprisingly called "the risk premium." Figuring out the risk premium is rather easy. It's any return above the "risk-free" rate you'd received on a U.S. Treasury bill, which is guaranteed by the full faith and credit of the U.S. government. (Well, virtually risk free, anyway.)

Being academics who know that history is a guide to future events, Fama and French claim that investors will only receive a 3 percent to 4 percent return above T-bills in the coming decades because stock returns are more likely to return to a long-term historical average, also prosaically called "reverting to the mean." That means stocks will return anywhere from 6 percent to 8 percent in the Fama/French model.

Robert Shiller, the Yale University economist who penned the bestseller *Irrational Exuberance* (Broadway Books, 2001)—the title is based on a pessimistic Alan Greenspan utterance—concurs with Fama and French for much the same reasons: "The evidence that stocks will always outperform bonds over long time intervals simply does not exist. Moreover, even if history supported this view, we should recognize (and at some level most people must recognize) that the future will not necessarily be like the past."

There are a number of reasons why the relentless surge of the postwar era may not continue. Stock-price increases are often a vestige of mass psychology. When the American public is mostly employed, making money and elevating its standard of living by buying things, corporate profits rise, which propels stock prices higher. If nobody bought—or felt they needed—Microsoft's products, for example, Microsoft would've gone the way of Western Union a while back. When consumers pull back, two-thirds of the economy retreats. That's what happens in a recession. Expectations are lower across the board and stock prices follow in lockstep. No corporate profit increases, no stock price ascent.

For all of the naysayers, however, there's an entire industry built on optimism, starting with Wall Street and its army of analysts. Author Harry Dent, a self-styled economist, for example, has made millions convincing people that the boom of the 1990s will extend into the first decades of the new millennium. His best-selling book *The Great Boom Ahead* (Hyperion, 1994) predicted that baby boomers will fuel unprecedented growth in the economy simply because they are in their peak spending years, which will be reflected in a surge in stock prices. Others joined the bandwagon of demographic prosperity, notably James Glassman and Kevin Hassett with their *Dow 36,000* (Times, 1999). While the Dow Jones Industrial Average keeps shrinking as I write this, there's little doubt that a bright future for the stock market was shared by millions in the ebullient 1990s.

More than one economist and market commentator, however, has fallen prey to the idea that they can predict which way a multitrillion-dollar economy will move and I won't venture it here. The only sure trait of market guessers is that they are consistently wrong. So it's still possible to believe that stock prices will continue to climb and build a case for stocks long term.

Don't Focus on Returns, Focus on Risk

Stock-market investing is a bit like stock-car racing. The fastest car doesn't win all of the time. It's the driver, assessing his risk at every turn, who wins by avoiding crashes and accelerating when he needs to in the straightaway. So investors who focused on swift returns in the past ran into trouble because they needed to pay more attention to *risk*. No matter how you view the short-term state of the economy or the markets, if you don't understand risk, you will be headed for a fall.

Doubtless, the manic devotion to returns has been inspired by four great years for the Standard & Poor's 500 Index (the "S&P 500" of the five hundred largest industrial companies, which is the benchmark index for blue-chip companies). From 1995 through 1999, the large companies that represent the S&P 500 had unprecedented earnings while cutting costs and improving productivity. So the idea of risk went out the door as millions of investors thought stocks were as safe as certificates of deposit (CDs). Here's what happened before the Icarus-like stock market fell to earth in March 2000:

THE END OF AN ERA?

Year	S&P 500 Return
1995	37.4%
1996	23.1%
1997	33.4%
1998	28.6%
1999	21.0%
5-Year Average	28.7%
75-Year Average	**11.0%**

As a result of the bull run of the mid- to late 1990s, many investors came to *expect* returns of 20 percent or more, ignoring the fact that the long-term average return for large stocks is 11 percent (since 1926). The outsized returns emboldened those who suddenly weren't satisfied with 20 percent returns to seek even greater returns in funds and stocks that were in the eye of the info-technology hurricane where the ego space is dead quiet, although it's surrounded by a raucous and risk-laden storm beyond the eye wall.

What happened to risk measurement during all of the market's gold-medal days? Although Wall Street was loath to take the surveys, I suspect millions didn't even consider risk, much less have a working understanding of how risk works in financial markets. Risk is like the mythical Hydra that Hercules slew. It has many heads and you need to consider each one before you plunge back into investing in markets that are unlikely to be as robust as the late 1990s. One of the best ways of charting risk is to profile the two ways of looking at mutual funds, which also applies to understanding categories of individual stocks.

The important lesson on risk and return is that the stock market can lose up to 43 percent in a given year, but if you stay invested over time, you can not only make that money back, you'll prosper. Every bear market—even the Depression—had an end that culminated in a rebound and higher stock prices. So the best approach to risk is often to stay put if you don't need your money within five years.

See the break out of the worst declines in the history of the market on page 12.

If you look at these years as snapshots of the stock market, the picture doesn't look too bright and gives you the impression that in any given year, you could lose money. While that's certainly true for investors who pull in and out of the market or "time" its many gyrations, the long-term record is one of recovery and growth (remember that 11 percent average annual return is over 75 years). So looking at one or two years of market history is misleading. The market is best understood by the kinds of risk you take and how long you have to invest.

TEN WORST DECLINES IN THE STOCK MARKET

Year	Decline*
1931	−43.3%
1937	−35.0%
1974	−26.5%
1930	−24.9%
1973	−14.7%
1941	−11.6%
1957	−10.8%
1966	−10.1%
1940	−9.8%
1962	−8.7%

*S&P 500 Index since 1926. *Source:* ICI.

How to Understand Types of Risk

Mutual funds, for example, are organized by the kind of vehicle they invest in and what they seek: growth (capital appreciation), income (from dividends or bond coupons), or a combination (total return). The most conservative and secure funds are pooling assets only for the purpose of providing short-term income, while the more sophisticated funds can switch between stocks and bonds according-ing to complex formulas. There are also different degrees of risk. For bond funds, there's interest-rate risk—the chance that interest rates will rise and depress bond prices (see the next chapter for a more detailed explanation of bond risk). If you are managing your own portfolio of individual stocks and bonds, you can look at single securities much the same way. They are subject to the same laws of risk depending on their type of business, how sensitive they are to movements in the economy or interest rates, and the quality of management.

For stock funds, you have *market* risk (the value on the stock exchange), *manager* risk (the manager picks the wrong stocks), *sector* risk (the sector falls out of favor with the market), and *opportunity* risk (the manager moves out of stocks into cash vehicles when the market rises). The following is a hierarchy of stock and bond funds from least risky to most risky. The higher you ascend in the list, the higher the potential for return or losing money.

FUND RISK HIERARCHY: LOWEST TO HIGHEST RISK

Type of Fund	Objective	Risk Level	Comment
Money-market fund	Short-term income	Lowest	Safe, sluglike
Short-term bonds	Income from bonds	Low	Income, slight risk
Intermediate-term bonds	Bond income	Moderate	More risk and yield
Mortgage	Income from mortgages	Moderate	Fairly steady income
International bonds	Overseas bonds	Moderate	More currency risk
Long-term bonds	Long-term income	High	Greatest market risk
Convertible bonds	Bonds may convert to stocks	High	Bond-stock chameleon
High-yield bonds	High-income corporate bonds	Highest	A tightrope
Stock funds			
Balanced funds	60% stocks, 40% bonds	Moderate	A two-humped camel
Equity-income funds	Income stocks, bonds	Moderate	A draft horse; steady
Growth and income funds	Primarily stocks, some bonds	Moderate	A little racier
International/world funds	Overseas stocks	Moderate	A walking horse
Growth stocks	All stocks	High	A greyhound
Aggressive growth stocks	Stocks promising high returns	Highest	A Thoroughbred
Sector funds	Stocks from one industry	Highest	A racing car

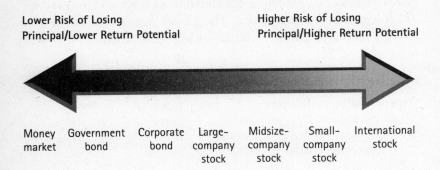

THE RANGE OF INVESTMENT PORTFOLIO RISKS
AND POTENTIAL RETURNS

Lower Risk of Losing
Principal/Lower Return Potential

Higher Risk of Losing
Principal/Higher Return Potential

| Money market | Government bond | Corporate bond | Large-company stock | Midsize-company stock | Small-company stock | International stock |

Risk by Style of Investing

Once you know how a fund invests (or single company, for that matter), the investment *style* of the manager becomes important in deciphering risk. When we refer to style in investing, we're not talking about Dior, Cardin, or DKNY. In stock funds, the two dominant schools are *growth* and *value* investing.

Growth managers buy companies that are growing their earnings and sales, which usually translate into higher stock prices. Value managers, in contrast, take a more measured approach by looking for companies that are selling at a discount to what they believe is the true market price. The dean of the value school is Warren Buffett, the chairman of the successful Berkshire Hathaway Inc., which acts like a mutual fund by buying other companies in whole or in part. Value managers are the bargain hunters of the market, while the growth managers are largely focused on how much a company is growing profits. A desirable growth company is increasing profits in the double-digit range every year. Both styles often overlap, however, in what is known as the "blend" style.

As you will discover in later chapters, the style of investing has a direct impact on risk. In a bear market when earnings are stagnant or declining, the value school often produces positive returns.

That's because the value players have picked companies that have little downside risk; the investments were already bought at rock-bottom prices and without a focus (exclusively) on earnings. It's like picking up a used car for a song and getting a few dents in it. You didn't pay much for it to begin with and you don't care what it looks like as long as the engine is sound. Value managers do extensive diagnostic tests on the engines of companies to see if they can run for years, whereas growth managers are more interested in how fast the cars can drive. In a bear market, value managers typi-cally outlast managers using growth styles of investing because they've done more homework on the durability of companies.

In examining risk, the style of investing is combined with the size or *capitalization* of the company. A large-company stock, for example, has a market capitalization of $10 billion and above. Market capitalization or "cap" is the current stock price times out-standing shares. There are the well-known "large caps" like General Motors, IBM, and Wal-Mart, which compete against the more than five thousand other listed stocks in the "mid-cap" (under $10 billion to about $1 billion) and small-cap (generally under $1 billion) categories. There's always a great deal of debate over where those cutoffs for capitalization should be, so I am approximating them.

Capitalization is important in measuring risk, although it's rarely seen that way. The smaller the company, the more unknowns there are. Nearly everyone can find out what Wal-Mart does. Just walk into any one of their thousands of stores and check out their goods. Smaller companies are less visible, undergo less scrutiny by Wall Street, and are often younger. Smaller companies also have a tougher time getting access to capital to expand and grow sales. On the positive side, smaller companies seem to weather downturns or high-inflation environments better than large companies because they have smaller operating expenses and tend to be more flexible when adjusting to market conditions and business cycles. So while your risk in the short term is greater with a small company, your overall returns over time are higher, on average, than with a larger company. From acorns, mighty oaks grow, the expression goes—if you've picked the right acorns. Small companies have plenty of room to grow if they have the right management.

This is how the matrix for capitalization and style works based on a system originally developed by Morningstar Mutual Funds:

STYLE AND SIZE MATTER

Style/Capitalization	Risk Level	Potential (Long-Term) Returns
Large-company growth	Moderate to high	Moderate
Large-company value	Low to moderate	Moderate
Mid-cap growth	Moderate	Moderate
Mid-cap value	Low to moderate	Moderate
Small-cap growth	Highest	Highest
Small-cap value	Moderate to high	Highest
Large-cap blend	Moderate	Moderate
Mid-cap blend	Moderate	Moderate
Small-cap blend	Moderate to high	Moderate to high
Multi-cap/blend(hybrids)	Moderate	Moderate

Ways of Measuring Risk

Since most market watchers are obsessed with performance and not risk, they routinely ignore the measures of risk that are critical in determining if specific funds are right for them. What really counts is *risk-adjusted return*, a number that tells you how well a fund did relative to a *risk-free* rate. If you were to plunk your money into U.S. Treasury bills, barring any cataclysmic political event or nuclear war, you would get back all of the money you invested in the T-bills plus a short-term rate of return. That's what academics refer to as a risk-free rate. Much of the foundation of risk analysis was laid down in the early 1950s by Harry Markowitz and William Sharpe, who were awarded Nobel Prizes in 1990 for their insights. They observed that investors had a natural inclination to chase returns instead of concentrating on how much risk they were taking to achieve those returns. Sound familiar? Risk is always a relative measure and it's measured in different ways:

Standard Deviation. This is not a pure measure of risk, but an indication of how much returns vary from an average, or *volatility*. If the standard deviation is 10 percent, then returns will either be 10 percent *higher* or 10 percent *lower* than that average. Often confused with risk, standard deviation is a measure of how much prices vary. It's a starting point in understanding risk. If a fund or stock has a high standard deviation, its price is all over the board. If you don't want the volatility, stay away from high standard deviations, which are quoted in every major fund rating service.

Beta. This number tells you how closely a fund tracks a market index. A beta of 1.0 means that the fund is doing everything the market is doing by matching the index. A beta of 1.20 means than the fund is 20 percent more volatile than the market. Again, volatility isn't necessarily risk in this case; it's correlation, so you need to go beyond beta. Nevertheless, you can often say that a fund or stock with a beta of less than 1.00 is likely to be less volatile than the larger market, although other risk factors apply.

R-Squared. This is an indirect way of measuring risk as it directly answers the question of how closely correlated this fund is to the market index. If you don't want a close correlation, that is, you want to diversify away from the market index, then you want a low R-squared. In terms of reducing overall risk, you want different kinds of investments in your portfolio that don't move the same way at the same time. When large stocks are down, for example, it's helpful to have other categories of investments that move up. Real estate, for example, typically moves in the opposite direction of stocks, so it's said to be *inversely correlated* or have a low R-squared. Once again, your best defense in a bear market is to have a variety of investments that don't move in lockstep.

Sharpe Ratio. Named after William Sharpe (page 16), this is a true measure of risk-adjusted returns because it combines standard deviation and "excess" returns that come above and beyond the risk-free rate of investing in T-bills. The higher the Sharpe Ratio, the higher the fund's risk-adjusted return over the past three years. A more elaborate risk-adjusted return system is employed by Morningstar Mutual Funds (see resources section or www.morningstar.com), which gives you a relative picture of risk versus the risk-free rate and how well similar funds performed. It's a useful enhancement of the Sharpe Ratio. In the Morningstar system, the higher the number of stars, the higher the risk-adjusted rating (five stars is highest). While both systems are hotly debated as to their veracity in determining risk, you need to look at some intangible measures (such as manager risk, personal risk tolerance, and time horizon risk) as well.

Manager Risk. This is an amalgam of different kinds of risks, to which, unfortunately, you can't assign a number because there are so many ways to evaluate managers. Some managers "turn over" their portfolios quite often—they buy and sell securities within the portfolio. If they are missing opportunities in the market by turning over the portfolio or jumping into cash by timing it, they may lower returns and add an element of risk. Other managers simply make bad guesses by plunging into the wrong sectors, for instance, health care instead of technology. With single companies, you can also incur *management risk*, the chance that executives running a corporation will make bad decisions that cost the company market share or profits, for instance, Motorola guessing wrong on digital cell phones and losing market leadership. So this is a huge factor in evaluating risk, but hard to measure or predict.

Personal Risk Tolerance. No risk-rating system is complete without first knowing what *your* risk level is, that is, how much of a loss or volatility you can tolerate in a year. If you see a standard deviation of 20, or the fund loses 30 percent or more in a year will you invest in it? The same thinking applies to a stock. The Morningstar system, for example, may give a fund a five-star risk-adjusted rating, but it can still have an awful year. All measures of risk look backward at historical returns, but you need to look at historical records (at least five years is a start) in determining what the worst-case scenario can be. The same applies to stocks. Can you sleep at night if a fund or stock is up 30 percent one year and down 30 percent the next?

Time Horizon Risk. And there's yet another level of risk to consider, *time horizon risk.* How long do you have to invest a given sum of money? This is most often ignored, but can be the most important risk factor of all. If it's one year, then your chances of losing it in the stock market vary from 17 percent to 40 percent, according to a Merrill Lynch survey. Over ten years, however, your risk of losing money in the stock market drops to zero (at least in the period measured from 1970 to 2000). As Richard Bernstein notes in *Navigate the Noise* (Wiley, 2001), "You can reduce the probability of a negative return by increasing your time horizon and increase it by decreasing your time horizon." Here are some guidelines:

Your Time Horizon:
When Do You Need the Money You're Investing?

1. If your focus is short-term (under five years), stay with the lowest-risk income vehicles (see next chapter). Your money is best invested in income vehicles, not stocks.

2. If your focus is long-term (five-plus years), and you know that you can accept up to 40 percent volatility in any given year, then you need to consider stock funds because of their superior returns relative to bonds and the fact that over any long period of time your chances of making money in stocks is very good. Even better, your chances of beating inflation in stock funds is 100 percent over time, which is what you need to beat the loss in purchasing power.

No measure of risk will tell you how a fund or company will perform in the future. A clue to risk is often provided by standard deviation and beta, but you have to combine that information with style, capitalization, five- to ten-year returns, and manager/management risk. Long-term returns (five years or more) are generally a good indicator of how a fund has performed in varying markets.

Ten-year returns are even better. Again, past performance doesn't predict future returns.

Better yet, just diversify, the magic theme that will enable you to make the right decision by owning a bit of each kind of company by style and capitalization, which I will explain in coming chapters. In the market meltdown of 2000, when 60 percent of stocks lost money, only 6 percent of diversified stock mutual funds were losers, so diversification through understanding of risk—not returns—is always your starting point.

The Long-Term, Diversified Approach

Given the historical record that stocks have always outperformed bonds and other financial assets in the long term, I can still recommend stocks as a primary vehicle of building wealth. Professor Jeremy Siegel of the University of Pennsylvania, author of *Stocks for the Long Run* (McGraw-Hill, 1998), is an ardent supporter of the view that long-term appreciation is only possible through stocks. Siegel's rationale is based on corporate profits expanding due to the growth of the global economy and the need to build everything from fiber-optic cable to power-generating plants. Profits go up because of global demand. Investors recognize the growth and invest in those companies, bidding up share prices further.

Siegel states that high stock values are justified if profits keep accelerating, inflation remains low, and capital gains taxes stay below 20 percent. All bets are off if we are in a long-term recession or war economy (both of which eventually end with a recovery). Nevertheless, I fully agree with Siegel that stock investing is still the way to long-term wealth with little risk—if you can stay invested over the next decade or so. You can't do it, however, by focusing on the short-term situation and trying to figure out where the "bottom" or "top" of the market is on any given day. That's a fool's errand, as Siegel points out:

> For most of us, trying to beat the market leads to disastrous results. We take far too many risks, our transactions

costs are high, and we often find ourselves giving in to the emotions of the moment—pessimism when the market is down and optimism when the market is high. Our actions lead to substantially lower returns than can be obtained by just staying in the market.

The keeper of the bible of long-term investing results, Ibbotson Associates, concurs with Siegel, although its *Stocks, Bonds, Bills, and Inflation Yearbook* is a bit more optimistic than the academics. The 2001 yearbook predicts a 100,000 Dow Jones industrial average by the year 2025 with large-company stocks growing at 13.5 percent a year; bonds will grow at a 5.7 percent rate.

If you need to beat inflation over time—and we *all* do—then stocks are likely to outperform all other classes of financial assets (bonds, money-market accounts, passbook savings, certificates of deposit). To achieve those higher returns, you need to take more risk, which, in the tumult of a bear market, is often forgotten as investors anguish over returns and losing money. You can be extremely creative, however, in what percentage and type of stocks, bonds, cash equivalents, and real estate you own to alter the *risk profile* of your portfolio. There are myriad ways of lowering risk and still staying ahead of inflation, which I'll discuss in coming chapters.

The real question is how to avoid being distracted by the constant dancing bubble bear reports of infinite wealth through unrealistic returns when you need to be focusing on risk. It's no easy task to avoid the second-by-second reports of the stock market. You can get stock quotes on your cell phone, trade in any market any time from your home computer, and monitor your portfolio for free. Even the most innocuous easy-listening radio station reports what happens on Wall Street, although it may have little or no bearing on your immediate life plans.

When the Bear Growls, You Can Move On

One day, shortly after the end of World War II, my great-aunt, Maria, was hanging up laundry on a clothesline in her backyard in a small town in Poland when Russian soldiers, who had occupied the country, came up to her and asked her to come to the village hall. My great-aunt asked if she could go back inside for a sweater, but the Russians insisted she wouldn't need one, as she wouldn't be gone long. She was taken to a railway yard and transported to a horrible prison camp. Her crime: She had married a German. Maria would have died in the camp, except that a woman next to her in the hospital gave my great-aunt her bread ration, which was only two grams. The woman died, but my great-aunt was released from the prison after several years. Upon arriving home, she found that her house was in shambles and that she didn't own it any more; other people were now living in her home.

After ten years of processing documents and visas, my great-aunt was allowed to visit her sister, my grandmother Elizabeth, who had come to the United States from Poland in the early part of the century. Upon visiting our 1,000-square foot, two-bedroom Cape Cod in Illinois, my great-aunt's first comment was "all this room for only one family?" She returned to Europe, and we never heard from her again.

My grandmother prospered in her own way. After raising three children as a single mother during the Great Depression, working as an overhead crane operator in a foundry during World War II, and running a metal lathe in a gear company after the war, she was able to provide a solid foundation for my father and two aunts. She was even able to save money to build her dream house in the country and grow tomatoes in her peaceful little garden. Although she never quite mastered English—she valiantly tried to teach Polish to my three brothers and me (learning it was like trying to eat sauerkraut with a knife)—she did fairly well in a predominantly male work environment until she was too ill to work and was "retired" by her employer.

I recall these stories every time I think about how wonderful it is to have a home, a community, and a country where you can enjoy the fruits of democracy and capitalism. Those who came before us worried about money, too, mostly because they came to the United States with only their body and soul. It's truly a blessing for us in this new century to be able to fret about mutual funds, stocks, bonds, real estate, and portfolio planning. So if you are worrying about your portfolio, find ways to reduce your risks and spend more time enjoying your life. You can learn most of what you need to know through this book (and the resources at the end of it). The mechanics of constructing a bear-proof portfolio are really quite simple. Once you absorb the basics of reducing risk and aiming for long-term returns, you will be able to enjoy your new prosperity with much less anxiety.

In the next few chapters, we'll walk through some ways of setting up your portfolio to reduce risk so that all you have to do is monitor it once a year and "bear proof" it as you see fit. I can see, however, that you are still watching the market and retirement-fund balance every day and your stomach is turning like a Tilt-A-Whirl. How do you ignore the "noise" and build a sustainable, risk-averse portfolio? You have to apply some discipline, as well as an understanding of risk and different investing management styles. There are a number of ways to make risk and bear markets work for you.

CHAPTER 2

Cash Is King, or Is It?
Short-Term Ways of Reducing Risk
and Finding Balance

Under ordinary circumstances, the safest way to keep fluid wealth is in the form of cash, although this is frequently unprofitable and inconvenient.

—Merryle Stanley Rukeyser

Bill Gross remembers his first job as a bond mutual fund analyst. He was making $11,000 a year in salary and wanted to be noticed by the chief executive of his company. He got a license plate with "Bonds1" on it and kept parking his car near the CEO's luxury sedan and even pulled up alongside the important man's car on occasion. Someone finally stopped him at a gas station when they noticed his license plate and asked him if he would bail a relative out of jail, thinking he was a bail bondsman. At that point, Gross relates, "It occurred to me that bonds *could* mean something else."

In Gross's sphere of influence, otherwise known as the fixed-income fund management world, he doesn't have any problem being recognized now. As a manager of more than $220 billion of fixed-income securities for Pacific Investment Management Company (PIMCO), he is probably the most successful bond fund manager on the planet (in terms of total return). His presence looms so large in the bond market that it's estimated that he and the funds he manages represent 1 percent of all of the bond assets in the United States. In the business for thirty-two years, his flag-ship PIMCO Total Return Institutional Fund has an 8.35 percent five-year annualized return, ranking it in the top tier of funds rated by Morningstar, the leading mutual-fund rating service. Over a ten-year period, the fund managed to deliver about 17 percent more return than similar funds, with nearly 15 percent less risk.

Gross's understanding of the delicate balance between risk and reward is what makes him (and his team) a manager who can outrun the worst traits of any market. Having had only one losing year in the last decade—when his fund was off a paltry 4 percent—he has one of the best long-term records of active bond-fund managers. What happened in the bad year (1994)? Alan Greenspan raised interest rates dramatically across the board to slow the economy, and the bond market was bruised badly. There's not much you can do in that kind of environment; when interest rates go up, bond prices go down. Investors are constantly chasing total return, so when new bonds pay a higher yield than old bonds, the old bonds become less desirable to investors and their prices drop. The opposite happens when interest rates fall. Investors love the existing or older bonds because they can lock in higher returns with little risk. It's a far cry from the days in 1967 when Gross set out to Las Vegas to make some money in blackjack and returned with $10,000 in his pocket.

Having been called the "Peter Lynch of bonds" (after the leg-endary manager of the Fidelity Magellan stock fund), Gross organ-izes his view on investing into two parts: structure and philosophy. Structure is what he calls a foundation, like the principle of a bank borrowing short-term and lending long-term. That's how they make money. Banks take your savings deposits, for example, and lend the money to people who want mortgages. This philosophy is anchored in being consistent and successful using simple strategies day in and day out.

Like most successful investors, Gross focuses on long-term results, not quarter-by-quarter gains. Although he admits that he is often transfixed watching CNBC, he says that you need a "road map that takes human emotion out of the investment equation. Emotion is a dangerous drug to investors."

Gross would agree that rampant emotions, or "irrational exuberance" in Greenspan's words, propelled the bubble market to new heights that may not be sustained in the future. He shares the view of Eugene Fama, Kenneth French, and Robert Shiller that the stock market will probably not produce double-digit returns in coming years and bonds may be very close to stocks in terms of returns with lower risk.

"We're moving into an age of diminished expectations," Gross told an adoring crowd at the Morningstar Mutual Fund Conference in Chicago in June 2001, where all of the leading mutual fund managers were invited by the fund-rating house to share their views on investing and the future. "There will be no more ten percent to fifteen percent returns in a more subdued economy. The problem was that the capitalistic ethic thrived on globalization, and technology [spending] went to excess. Bubbles were produced in the NASDAQ market, telecommunications, and consumption. We simply overdid it and bought stocks at too-high prices. We're in the process of deflating bubbles, that's what capitalists do. We are now headed toward a period of adjustment and diminished results."

Gross's pronouncement was probably not well received, although his wisdom on the markets is noted throughout the world. Was his speech a hallmark announcing a coming age of lower returns after a bacchanal of excessive profits and market returns? If Gross is right—and he certainly can be as wrong as most economists are when predicting the economy's future direction—then this may have been his "irrational exuberance" moment, an official signal that we're heading into a single-digit world of total return. It is always difficult to gauge how money managers receive a message like this, although most of them discount it, knowing that world events can make the market turn in a moment. Of the thousand or so managers in attendance at Morningstar, perhaps one of the most important pow-wows of the year for professional money runners, only a handful will go back to their clients and say, "Guess what Bill Gross said: Returns are going to be down across the board." Many of the larger fund houses (those managing more than $10 billion) will be cautious in their newsletters and issue gentle warnings that "past performance doesn't predict future results." They have to do that. Gross is not a voice in the wilderness, however, because he offers a solid case for why returns may be lower and the risks that accompany that prediction.

Noting an often-overlooked fact that during the last market run-up a huge amount of fiber-optic cable was installed throughout North America and 95 percent of this infrastructure is not being utilized—one indicator of a bubble economy—Gross goes on to state his case: "The economy [in the form of the Gross Domestic Product (GDP)] *can't* expand at four percent to five percent a year: maybe it will grow at two percent. Corporate profit growth mimics GDP, so you can't expect corporate profits to grow more than two percent. That means about a five percent return on stocks. Double-digit returns can no longer be with us over time."

Are Bonds a Safer Bet in a Low-Return Environment?

Gross's forecast really hinges on the issue of sustainability. Are double-digit returns a way of life for stocks or not, and if they're not, what does a bear market entail? Would it be more prudent to retreat to bonds and maintain a secure, lower-risk return? Again, history suggests that double-digit returns are highly unusual in the modern era. Ibbotson Associates has tracked stocks, bonds, and inflation since the 1920s and notes that the 28.7 percent average return on large- and small-company stocks achieved in the 1990s is unprecedented and unlikely to be sustained. In only four decades since the 1920s have there been double-digit returns in stocks— the 1920s, 1950s, 1980s, and 1990s. Each decade of heady growth was followed by either a crash or two decades of mediocre single-digit growth. Here's a breakdown:

- After the crash of 1929, the 1930s produced a −0.1 percent return in large-company stocks and double-digit growth wasn't seen again until the 1950s, when large-company stocks had their best year, posting a 19.4 percent average return.
- After the relatively low inflation and corporate growth in the

1950s, the 1960s and 1970s were plagued by inflation and the Vietnam War and were subpar decades for the stock market, turning in 7.8 percent and 5.9 percent returns, respectively.

▪ Once the Vietnam War ended, gas shortages and oil embargoes went away, and inflation was tamed by an aggressive Federal Reserve, the 1980s and 1990s witnessed explosive growth with 17.5 percent and 18.2 percent returns, respectively.

Source: Stocks, Bonds, Bills, and Inflation: 2001 Yearbook, 2001 Ibbotson Associates, Inc. Based on copyrighted works by Ibbotson and Sinquefield. All rights reserved. Used with permission.

If one sees a pattern developing—and this is a dangerous business when predicting the stock market—Gross may be right about a single-digit decade and his forecast may not be a jeremiad. As an investor, the twin titans of inflation and corporate profits loom large, and how those two factors play out will ultimately determine whether stocks or bonds will prevail. High inflation will boost bond yields, but you have to subtract inflation from the yield to get the *real* return. Inflation is the Loki of investing, almost always disguised and never seen, ready to spoil any party and deceive the most honest of savers. Stocks can prevail in times of higher inflation, but again, their returns only slightly outpace bonds.

Should inflation remain low and Gross turn out to be wrong about receding corporate profits, then his forecast of lower stock returns will be inaccurate. If history is correct, however, then the era of reduced expectations is upon us.

Cash and Bonds in a Lower-Return Environment

You will drive yourself mad trying to predict what's going to happen to the economy, and thankfully your investing strategies don't require a crystal ball, so don't worry about it. Let's look at your short-term picture first and deal with stocks later. All you need to focus on now is: (1) how long you have to invest for each of your investment goals, that is, determining your time-horizon risk; and (2) how much risk you want to take. If you are planning for retirement, you'll be better able to meet your goals if you have more than a ten-year time horizon for investment returns. You can take more risk because your portfolio will outgrow bear markets. If your savings goals are less than five years away, then you need to have a good cash management strategy.

Cash is a fairly simple concept but misunderstood by most investors. Traditionally, cash has been seen as money in a checking or passbook account. Broadly defined, it's money invested in easily liquidated vehicles such as money-market mutual funds, money-market deposit accounts (through banks), Treasury bills, notes, bonds, and other *debt securities* such as corporate notes. Cash, even currency, represents a promise. Look at a dollar bill. On the very top (above the "United States of America") is the line "Federal Reserve Note." The dollar bill is a promise to pay you—or whoever you give it to—a dollar's worth of something. It's like a little bond. In the past, you could redeem currency for gold or silver, but that policy vanished in the 1970s when the government decided to back our money with credit. So backing up that promise is the full faith and credit of the U.S. government, or in this case, the Federal Reserve Bank, which authorizes the U.S. Treasury to print the money.

Cash is liquid, meaning you can get it from an ATM or from your checking account, write a check from your money market account, or transfer money from another account where you needn't pay a penalty or involve a broker. You can put it in your pocket, hand it to your significant other, or take it to the casino to buy chips. As an immediate promise to pay a debt, your dollar also says, "This note is legal tender for all debts, public and private." This little phrase, on every bill the Treasury prints, means you can use it for anything. Just as cash is liquid, stocks and real estate are *illiquid*. You can't just hand over the title to your home to pay off a debt (although that's what happens if you don't pay off a home-equity loan). You have to line up a real estate agent or broker to sell the home and redeem its cash value minus closing costs, taxes, and commission. There are similar problems with a stock certificate. You have to trade it through a market using a broker and clearing-house to redeem its market value.

Because of its liquidity and portability, cash is best for short-term debts. Having all of your short-term needs sitting in currency is impractical and creates a storage and security problem for most people. That's why there are a number of vehicles to store cash and give you a return in exchange for the use of your money. The following cash vehicles or "equivalents" are worth considering and are listed from safest to riskiest:

CASH AND BOND FUNDS

Vehicle	Relative Safety
Cash Equivalents	
NOW checking accounts	Secure with FDIC protection
U.S. Treasury bill	Full faith and credit guarantee
Money-market deposit account	FDIC insured
Money-market mutual fund	Mostly secure
Certificate of deposit	FDIC insured*
Bonds	
U.S. inflation bonds (TIPS)	Secure[†]
U.S. Treasury note	Moderate[‡]
Short-term bond mutual fund	Moderate
Intermediate bond fund	Moderate
Ginnie Mae government bonds	Moderate[§]
Short-term corporate fund	Moderate
Intermediate-term bonds	Moderate
Municipal bonds	Moderate
Zero-coupon bonds	High volatility
Long-term corporate bonds	High risk and return
High-yield corporate bonds	Highest risk
U.S. 20-year Treasury bond	Secure if held to maturity*

*Since the longer the maturity, the more interest-rate risk you incur, bonds with a longer maturity have more risk if interest rates rise. A certificate of deposit is risk-free unless not insured by the Federal Deposit Insurance Corporation and presents some risk because it can't be redeemed before its maturity without paying a penalty, so you may lose the opportunity to get a higher return elsewhere.

The Subtle Risks of Bonds

The understanding of risk is central to determining how to invest in cash equivalents and bonds. You'll get your most secure return or principal in money-market accounts, certificates of deposit (CDs), Treasury bills, and anything insured by the FDIC. In these vehicles, your principal (what you put in) is guaranteed, along with the interest (in most cases). So if you need this money to pay bills every month or are saving for a big downpayment on something (house, car, boat, college), these vehicles will serve you well and pose *no credit* or *default* risk, the chance that they won't pay you back your full principal. Since the FDIC and U.S. Treasury have consistently backed up their promises with the deep pockets of the American taxpayer, there's little need to worry about losing money on T-bills or CDs that are insured.

With corporate bonds, there are several services that rate the issuer's financial security to give you an idea of the chance of default risk. This rating system is based on letter grades, with "AAA" being the highest and "unrated" being the lowest. Bond defaults in the corporate world are relatively rare, however, unless you plunge into the world of "high yield" or "junk" bonds, which pay nearly double-digit yields in exchange for a high risk of default. Junk bonds typically carry the lowest ratings from bond-rating houses.

The most pernicious risk for bond investors is *interest-rate* or *market* risk. As I've noted, if interest rates rise, bond prices drop as investors scramble to lock in higher yields of newly issued bonds and dump the lower-yielding issues. Interest-rate risk is not a problem

---

† Bonds issued by the U.S. Treasury that will pay you extra interest based on the rise in inflation. ‡ Government bonds have no interest-rate risk if held to maturity. § GNMA bonds, or "Ginnie Maes," represent mortgages that have been pooled together into notes. As such, these bonds carry a unique risk called "pre-payment risk," or the chance that homeowners will refinance at lower rates when interest rates decline. That reduces the yield (your return) on Ginnie Maes and market prices.

with single bonds you hold to maturity. You will normally get all of your principal back plus interest. Bond mutual funds and bonds that you sell before maturity have the greatest exposure to interest-rate risk. *The general rule is the longer the maturity, the greater the risk.* Before you invest, you need to ask a bond-fund manager what the average maturity or duration of the portfolio is.

If you are investing for short-term goals in a portfolio with long-term bonds (those with maturities of six years or more), you are taking a chance of losing some of your principal when interest rates rise. A useful measure of bond-fund risk is called *duration*, which is based on average maturity. Let's say the duration of a bond fund is 5, which means the average maturity of the bonds within the portfolio is about five years. If interest rates rise 1 percent, then you stand the chance of *losing* 5 percent of your principal. The higher the duration, the greater the exposure to interest-rate risk. So if your savings goal is five years or less, stick with money-market funds, short-term bond funds, or intermediate-term bonds. Stay away from long-term bonds unless you need a high current yield now and are willing to switch to short-term funds if rates rise. You can also "ladder" your portfolio with CDs and bonds with increasing maturities (from one year to twenty years) to reduce interest-rate risk.

Bonds also carry subtle risks that are often ignored by most investors. If you lock your money into a CD or Treasury note for five years, you risk the *opportunity* of getting a higher return in another investment, namely another bond or stock. This opportunity risk is predicated on your willingness to sacrifice return for absolute safety of your principal. Opportunity risk also comes into play when you lock your money into a bond and interest rates rise. You lose out on the chance to be in a higher-yielding bond, which is why bond prices fall when interest rates rise.

Say you want safe and secure bonds. A natural choice would be EE U.S. Savings Bonds, which are available at 50 percent discount to face value (i.e., a $100 bond can be bought for $50) and earn interest for up to thirty years. These bonds pay 90 percent of a five-year Treasury note's interest and compound semiannually (4.07

percent as this went to press). Unfortunately, your bonds wouldn't reach the face value of $100 for seventeen years and the interest rate could fall behind inflation. You could do better—and have a more liquid bond—elsewhere.

To partially eliminate the opportunity risk in the short term, stay in a *money-market mutual fund* that is actively managed to chase the highest short-term rates, or vehicles that pay "market" rates of interest from bonds maturing in less than a year. Of course, if short-term interest rates fall—as they did throughout 2001—your money-market yields will decline as well. This *income* risk is unavoidable in money-market funds, which are managed to track short-term interest rates, although your principal will be safe.

MATCH YOUR TIME HORIZON TO THE RISK OF THE VEHICLE

Savings Goal	Savings Vehicle
Short-term/under 1 year	Money-market funds, T-bills, CDs
Mid-term/1–3 years	CDs, TIPS,* T-notes, short-, intermediate-term bonds
Longer-term/3–5 years	Intermediate bonds, I-bonds, Corporate bonds, GNMAs
Beyond 5 years	Balanced stock and equity income funds (see chapter 3)

*A U.S. Treasury inflation-protected bond.

How to Manage Cash for Low Risk

First, forget about yields and figure out *when* you'll need the cash. Then, determine the risk you can afford to take given your time horizon. If you have a son or daughter entering college next year, for example, you can't afford to have that money sitting in a twenty-year bond, and certainly not in the stock market. A money market fund or CD that matures when the tuition is due is probably your best choice. Keep in mind that you can buy Treasury bonds directly from the government or through a mutual fund. See page 33 for some guidelines.

If savings yields stay low (under 5 percent), you will want to ask yourself how much more risk you can take to get a higher return. It pays to shop around for the highest money-market rates. The most competitive money-market mutual funds charge no management fees or nominal ones (under .20 percent a year; see www.imoneynet.com for pointers to these funds), so your return is higher. As in all of the other investment vehicles I'll discuss in this book, *always look for the lowest management fees you can find.* That's an easy way of boosting returns that doesn't involve taking on more risk.

There are several variations of short-term bond funds in the mutual-fund business. The "ultra-short" bond funds are just one step ahead of money-market funds and may invest in securities that mature in two years or less. There are also inflation-adjusted bond funds that offer slightly more return (see page 36 for more details). Such vehicles offer a portfolio of inflation-adjusted Treasury bonds or "TIPS." When the rate of inflation—the government calls it the Consumer Price Index—rises, you get a little extra return added on.

Why You Should Own Bonds at All If, in the End, Stocks Are Better Long Term

Bonds are essential to "bear-proof" investing because they pay income and their prices (for short- and intermediate-maturity bonds) don't move as dramatically in either direction as stock prices. Risk-averse investors prefer bonds, especially when they are spooked by incredible volatility in the stock market. For example, the lowest average standard deviation (SD) or volatility for bonds was back in the 1920s, according to Ibbotson data. Intermediate-term government bonds then had on SD of 1.7 percent; the SD for T-bills was just 0.3 percent. Contrast that to the highest average SD recorded for small-company stocks in the 1930s—78.6 percent—and you have a good idea of why investors love bonds in rough times.

As a further example, even blue-chip large-company stocks are volatile when compared to bonds. SDs for large-company stocks have never posted in the single digits, ranging from 13.1 percent in the 1970s (an awful decade for stocks overall) to 41.6 percent in the 1930s (the worst decade). In contrast, the most volatile period for bonds was in the 1980s, mostly because inflation raged in double digits the first few years of the decade, until it was finally restrained to under 5 percent at the end of the decade. That inflation resulted in SDs of 14.1 percent and 16 percent for long-term corporate and government bonds, respectively, according to Ibbotson. Bonds can be volatile, but not as much as stocks.

You must also consider the nagging reality of inflation and taxes. No matter how many ways you shake the dice, bonds might track inflation, but they won't outpace it. Stocks can generally out-perform the rate of inflation; real estate sometimes does. Inflation is the ogre under the bridge when it comes to your portfolio. It's another form of risk that particularly ravages bond funds. If you were to take what you perceive as the safest-possible approach—100 percent money-market and short-term bond funds—you would still be incurring inflation risk because your purchasing power would be consistently eroded over time and your bonds would never outperform the rate of inflation. Once you add in taxes, you definitely lose money. The following table illustrates how inflation diminishes your investments:

THE OGRE UNDER THE BRIDGE: INFLATION OVER TIME

Over this time . . .	$1,000 will be worth . . .
5 years	$897
15 years	$722
25 years	$580
35 years	$467

Based on 2.2% annual rate of inflation, a historically low rate since inflation has averaged about 3% over the past 75 years. *Source:* Investment Company Institute.

TREASURY BONDS THAT MATCH INFLATION

If you just want to keep pace with inflation, the U.S. Treasury offers "inflation-protected" securities (TIPS) that make a small interest premium based on the prevailing consumer price index. While you won't outrun inflation over time, these "full faith and credit" bonds will preserve your money in the short term. Bonds are issued at face value in denominations from $50 to $10,000 and earn a fixed rate of return plus a semiannual inflation rate up to 30 years. For more information, call the Treasury Department, which sells them directly, at (800) 943-6864 or (202) 874-4000, or visit the agency on-line at www.publicdebt.treas.gov.

How Much Should You Invest in Bonds in Rough Times?

If bonds are such a quiet harbor in times of trouble, why are long-term investors so smitten with stocks? Why not retreat to bonds every time the market becomes volatile, which is, actually, most of the time? Stocks outperform bonds simply because investors are willing to pay a premium for the additional risk and higher rewards and because stock prices are based on corporate earnings, which have generally risen faster than inflation over time. Here's the standard comparison of returns for stock funds:

THE HISTORICAL RECORD: STOCKS PERFORM BETTER
THAN BONDS OVER TIME

Investment Type	Average Return	Range*	Period Covered
Emerging market stocks	13.4%	37.3% to −16.7%	11 years
Foreign stocks	13.2%	58.4% to −8.7%	30 years
Large stocks	11.4%	43.4% to −42.4%	74 years
Small stocks	12.6%	88.9% to −51.9%	74 years
Real estate	12.0%	33.5% to −10.5%	28 years
Long-term T-bonds	5.1%	35.4% to −6.0%	74 years
30-day T-bills	3.8%	12.6% to 0%	74 years

*This table, however, tends to be misleading because it tracks investments over different time periods and only reflects economy-wide averages within each type. For example, emerging market and foreign stock funds haven't been around very long compared to large-company stocks, so there's not as much historical data. Who knows what foreign and emerging markets did in the 1930s, '40s, and '50s? The most credible information exists on large- and small-company stocks and bonds. Those numbers, however, are also averages of a large group of stocks and don't reflect individual mutual fund performance. Internet stock mutual funds had returns ranging from 200% to −90% over the past two years, so an average doesn't give you a perfect picture of the volatility of stocks and stock funds. *Source: Mutual Funds* magazine.

The only glaring truth from this deceptive array of numbers is that if you keep your money entirely in T-bills—or cash—you'll definitely have the lowest possible volatility and risk, but you'll also lose money because you have to subtract inflation (about 3 percent over the last seventy-five years) and taxes. Cash is strictly a short-term instrument to pool money and not a viable alternative to stocks in the long run.

Of course, that begs the question: How much should you have in cash and bonds? The old rule used to gauge your allocation to your age. That is, the older you got, the more you needed in cash and bonds. Since people are living to be much older than when that strategy was first hatched (octogenarians and centenarians are the fastest-growing demographic groups), the focus now is on beating inflation long term and not *outliving* your money. Ask yourself:

INFLATION ERODES GROWTH—
BUT STOCKS HAVE OUTPACED IT*

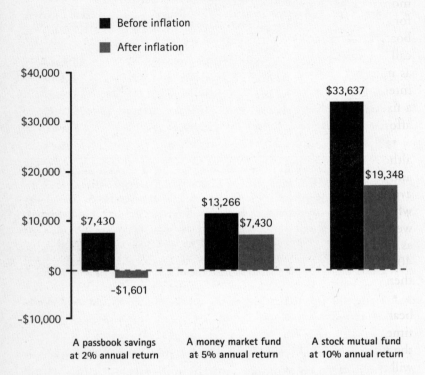

■ Before inflation

■ After inflation

*Assumes $5,000 invested over 20 years and 3% inflation. The returns in the above chart are hypothetical. *Source:* Ariel Capital Management.

• Can you tolerate the risk of losing up to 40 percent of your nest egg after a bad year (or years) in the stock market? If not, stick with bonds and a lower percentage of stocks—less than 60 percent in stocks in your total portfolio. (More on this in chapter 3). A 100 percent stock portfolio returned about 11 percent between 1926 and 2000, with −43.1 percent being the worst one-year loss during that period. A 60 percent stocks, 40 percent bonds portfolio had a 9.4 percent return, with a worst-year loss of −26.6 percent.

▪ How much time do you need before you will start withdrawing money? This question isn't solely predicated on needing money for retirement. As I mentioned earlier, you may be saving for college bills, a down payment on a second (or first) home, a boat, home remodeling, or your "third age" (retirement, or what I call "new prosperity"). If your goal is less than five years away, keep as much of the money in low-risk cash equivalents and short- to intermediate-term bonds. This is the easy part since you are saving a fixed amount of money for a definite period of time. You can't afford to lose principal, so don't take the risk.

▪ Do you want to wait out a down market? Some investors do, although they can never be quite sure when the bear market begins and ends. The classic definition of a bear market is when the stock averages are down at least 20 percent. Here's the hitch: it depends which stocks you are watching. The NASDAQ, which is heavily weighted with smaller technology companies, was down 30 percent as 2001 came to a close. If you can't sleep at night and are seeing your 401(k) dollars jumping over fences like sheep into the jaws of wolves, then keep some assets in cash, money-market funds, and CDs.

▪ How patient are you, really? The market does rebound from bear markets, it just takes time (see the table on page 40). Over time, though, as I mentioned in chapter 1, the longer you stay in the market, the lower your risk, and the lower the chance that you will miss heady gains. If you have the time to wait, your investment will recover during a stock rebound.

You probably noticed I'm only going back forty-five years and not including the 1930s. That's because the depression is a special case. If we hit another major Dust Bowl depression, all bets are off. In the postwar era, the good news is that the longest investors have had to wait for a rebound is about three and a half years and, on average, they've recovered in nineteen months. If you can stomach losing from half to one-third of your capital in the short term—and then rebounding—then stocks can comprise a majority of your portfolio, *provided* your income needs and short-term savings goals are met.

WHEN THE BEAR STOPS GROWLING, PATIENCE PAYS OFF: MARKET DECLINES AND TIME NEEDED TO RECOVER AND BREAK EVEN

Market Peak	Market Low	Total Drop	Break-even Period
8/2/56	10/22/57	−22%	2 years
12/12/61	6/26/62	−28%	17 months
2/9/66	10/7/66	−22%	15 months
11/29/68	5/26/70	−36%	27 months
1/11/73	10/3/74	−48%	45 months
9/21/76	3/6/78	−20%	4 months
11/28/80	8/12/82	−27%	23 months
8/25/87	12/24/87	−34%	21 months
7/16/90	10/11/90	−20%	9 months
7/17/98	8/31/98	−28%	19 months
Average		**−28%**	**19 months**

Source: T. Rowe Price.

One of the best reasons for not having all of your money in the bond market is that stock investors consistently overreact to any and all kinds of news. So events that may seem negative cause huge declines and boom times produce the outsized rally we witnessed from 1991 through 1999. Benjamin Graham, the father of value investing, often noted that "everyone knows that speculative stock movements are carried too far in both directions . . . thus it seems that any intelligent person, with a good head for figures, should have a veritable picnic in Wall Street, fattening off other people's foolishness."

Yet another scenario emerges if a recession produces deflation and interest rates continue to fall. Falling interest rates are good for every part of the economy because they reduce the cost of credit and doing business. Your mortgage rate drops and big corporations pay less for financing their debt. Businesses can increase their profit margins and stock prices go up. And bond prices rise in lockstep. In studying down markets, John Rothchild observed in *The Bear Book* (Wiley, 2000), "Stocks and bonds do well together. This happens when interest rates are falling and inflation is under control, a double benefit investors have enjoyed from 1982 to 1997." This is one of the strongest arguments for a portfolio that includes stocks and bonds. In recessions, where the economy contracts—and there's little or no inflation—a mix of 60 percent stocks and 40 percent bonds will probably beat the bear long term.

Bond Funds Worth Considering

There are a number of well-managed bond funds that deserve your attention. I've grouped them according to risk and return—the lower the return, the lower the risk, which is perfect for short-term goals. In addition to choosing high-quality funds to improve your investments, you can boost your return by buying "no-load" funds (no sales charge) with the lowest-possible expenses. That means *not* buying a bond fund through a broker or bank. Sales charges and high expenses lower your returns, which are not all that high to begin with, so avoid them.

BOND FUNDS

Fund	5-year return	Minimum $	Phone
Above-average risk			
Fidelity Investment Grade	7.30%	$ 2,500	(800) 544-8888
Loomis Sayles Bond Ret.	6.13%	$25,000	(800) 633-3330
Vanguard High-Yield Corp.	4.63%	$25,000	(800) 662-7447
Moderate risk			
Harbor Bond	8.11%	$ 2,000	(800) 422-1050
Vanguard Total Bond Index	7.76%	$10,000	(800) 662-7447
FPA New Income	7.68%	$ 1,500	(800) 982-4372
Low risk			
Strong Advantage Inv.	5.39%	$ 2,500	(800) 368-1030
PIMCO Short-Term A	5.67%*	$ 2,500	(888) 877-4626
Vanguard Prime	2.08%†	$ 3,000	(800) 662-7447

Returns (annualized) through 12/31/01. *3-year return only. Returns do not reflect current yields. †Current 7-day yield as of 1/10/02. *Source:* Morningstar.

Once you've met your short-term needs with the appropriate bond funds, you need to focus on longer-term goals, and that's when the art of portfolio management becomes a real chore. What percentage of stocks to bonds do you need to achieve a decent return? What kinds of stocks and bonds do best in a down market? Can you effectively mix stocks and bonds to attain a low-risk balance that blends returns that will outlast a bad year overall for stocks?

It's simplest to answer the last question first: yes. That's what the next chapter is about. Before I step into that realm, I'd like to leave you with the idea that cash and bonds—no matter how Bill Gross describes the future and the state of the economy—are expressions, wishes, promises. In the words of James Buchan, who eloquently penned *Frozen Desire: The Meaning of Money*:

> The difference between a word and a piece of money is that money has always and will always symbolize different things to different people: a banknote may describe to one person a drink in a pub, a fairground ride to another, to a third a diamond ring, an act of charity to a fourth, relief from prosecution to a fifth and, to a sixth, simply to sensations of comfort or security. For money is incarnate desire. Money takes wishes, however vague or trivial or atrocious, and broadcasts them to the world, like the Mayday of a ship in difficulties."

Something to think about the next time you pick up a dollar bill, a savings bond, or your money-market statement. When they say people lust after money, they are telling the truth. This desire, however, can be channeled and disciplined so that we are not practicing unsafe money management.

CHAPTER 3

A Balanced Approach to Risk: Stocks, Bonds, and Real Estate in Perspective

To the ecological mind, balance of nature has merits and also defects. Its merits are that it conceives of a collective total, that it imputes some utility to all species, and that it implies oscillations when balance is disturbed. Its defects are that there is only one point at which balance occurs, and that balance is normally static.

—Aldo Leopold

It always strikes me how much the science of ecology has to teach people managing money. There's a reason why the language is so similar. Economies and ecosystems are viewed as systems. Markets rise, fall, and "correct." There can be "order imbalances" when there are too many buy and sell orders in the market (they must always be equal). Stocks can occupy niches or sectors the way animals find a niche in the food chain. The bear is a large predator, a mammal. The bull is a vegetarian, a ruminant. Is it any surprise that the two directions of the market are characterized as large animals occupying specific niches?

It's not a coincidence that ecology and economy have the same Greek root: *oikos*, which means household. *Oikonomia*, or economy, is the management of a household, whereas *oikologia*, or ecology, is the study of the household. Managing households involves money. Managing nature, which does a fair job of it on her own, involves natural resources and energy. Both systems also involve a need for equilibrium or balance. If you don't have enough money to maintain your house or household, your house will deteriorate and you'll have to move as it becomes uninhabitable or possibly condemned. In the natural system, too much rain, sun, volcanic activity, predation, and a host of other elements can drastically alter that system. And so it goes with the balance of stocks and bonds.

Like animals occupying niches in a food chain, stocks and bonds compete with all other assets that produce a tangible total return. Since it's hard to gauge what real estate, gold, gemstones, paintings, and other collectibles are worth year to year, their tangible worth can't be fairly compared with stocks and bonds (although we'll be examining real estate shortly). Rational investors are always trying to get the best return on their money, so they oscillate between stocks and bonds to get that return.

From the beginning of 2000 through mid-2001, when bonds outperformed stocks for the first time in more than twenty years, investors fled the uncertain and decidedly negative returns of stocks and found refuge in bonds. It was like a stampede of animals running away from a wildfire, seeking the relative safety of a placid lake. Those who switched completely out of stocks and into bonds were rewarded. From January 1, 2001, through December 31, 2001, stocks (as measured by the benchmark S&P 500) dropped 12 percent versus 7.05 percent for bonds (as measured by the Lehman Brothers U.S. Aggregate Index, a breadbasket of domestic bonds). It also helped the bond market that investors had been selling their stocks because of awful earnings reports and dropping interest rates. But markets change overnight. The people who switched were either professional money managers or just plain lucky.

It's an oversimplification to say you can easily "run" from one asset to another. Professionals and amateurs alike are notoriously inaccurate in timing the move from stocks to bonds and vice versa.

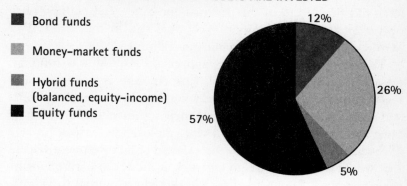

HOW MUTUAL FUND ASSETS ARE INVESTED

■ Bond funds

▨ Money-market funds

■ Hybrid funds
(balanced, equity-income)
■ Equity funds

12%

26%

5%

57%

Source: Investment Company Institute, 2000.

Despite the blather on television, no analyst or money manager knows precisely when the market will turn. If you guess wrong—and most people do—you lose out on the higher returns in stocks when you flee to bonds (especially when you miss a stock rebound). The opposite and riskier course is staying in stocks far too long and not taking losses to accept a reasonably safe yield in bonds. Can you find a middle ground that avoids these common mistakes? Funds that balance a mix between stocks and bonds are likely choices to achieve a lower-risk profile and garner returns from both markets.

Balanced Funds: The Middle Ground

For Chris Brown, managing the $1.2 billion Pax World Balanced Fund of stocks and bonds is a family business. Comanaging with Robert Colin since October 2001, he took the reins of Pax World Balanced Fund from his father, Anthony, who stepped down in April 1998. Tony Brown had managed the fund since its inception in 1971, a year in which most Americans had not yet heard of mutual funds, didn't invest in the stock market and were still getting over the break-up of the Beatles. The end of the Vietnam War and the advent of the personal computer, cell phones, fiber optics, and the World Wide Web were still in the future. Pax World even predates the first stock index fund.

Tony Brown was asked to manage the Pax World fund by founders Luther Tyson and Jack Corbett, who wanted a socially responsible fund that would attract capital from religious groups. Tyson and Corbett used to spend their summers in Portsmouth, New Hampshire, where Brown was employed as a stock broker. "We started talking about how there should be an investment vehicle that would allow churches to invest their money in harmony with their message," Brown recalls. "We thought a mutual fund with social criteria would do that, so we started Pax."

When Pax, which means "peace" in Latin, started up, there were 670 mutual funds in existence. Only a small percentage of the middle class invested in stocks—or knew anything beyond the classic "blue chips": IBM, GM, and Procter & Gamble. Today there are more than 9,000 mutual funds and a whole category of funds that use socially responsible investment (SRI) criteria. There are now funds targeted to Catholics, Lutherans, and Muslims; funds that focus on clean, environmentally sustainable energy; and funds that eschew investments in tobacco, gambling, alcohol, and employee-hostile companies.

The group known as "SRI investors" now boasts of more than $1 trillion in assets, most of that invested through institutions and pension funds. Since SRI investors as a whole tend to scrutinize companies in greater detail, they often find corporate managers who are durable, are consistent, and produce profits in varying market conditions. It's not unusual for "social" funds to outperform their respective peers because they dissect stocks to the nth degree and unearth many long-term winners.

SRI FUNDS BALANCE RETURNS

- There are 192 mutual funds that screen using SRI or environmental principles, totaling $103 billion in assets, according to Weisenberger, Inc.
- Domestic SRI funds returned an average 12.32% over the past five years, besting the average U.S. stock fund at 11.34%. Despite their rigorous social screens, many SRI funds invest in high-growth technology companies, which tend to have better environmental records than older "blue chips."
- SRI funds generally don't invest in, or "screen out," companies that are in the business of producing weapons, liquor, nuclear power, or gambling services.
- They also try to avoid companies with a poor environmental protection history and seek out those with progressive policies on hiring and promoting women and minorities. SRI fund managers also like to promote community development, clean energy, and international development.

Under Chris Brown, the Pax World Balanced Fund invests from 65 percent to 70 percent in stocks and the remainder in bonds. Balanced funds typically start out with a 60 percent/40 percent stocks-to-bonds mix and change that percentage depending on market conditions. The only constant is that although these funds maintain a heavier weighting in stocks than bonds, all of them hold bonds as a cushion in case the stock market goes south. Pax World Balance maintains at least 25 percent of its portfolio in bonds, so that it's never "fully invested" in the stock market.

Also called "total return," "hybrid," or "all-weather" funds, balanced funds are the friendly mixed breed of mutual funds. They have neither the volatility nor the risk of pure stock funds, so they tend to do better in down markets than funds that hold no bonds. The best balanced fund managers, like Brown, make small guesses on where the better *values* are, that is, whether stocks or bonds are priced fairly relative to their respective markets or each other. As you can see below, over short periods of time, which include the year 2000, balanced funds offer a better return than growth funds. Longer term, however, the two kinds of funds pull even:

BALANCED FUNDS VERSUS GROWTH-STOCK FUNDS

	3-year Return	5-year Return
Balanced funds	3.8%	11%
Growth funds	-3.0%	11%

Annualized returns through 6/30/01. *Source:* Lipper.

Balanced funds provide many investors with an "all-in-one" investment strategy. Otherwise you need to make risky choices on asset allocation—choosing the right percentage and the right type or style of stocks and bonds. This is a delicate business fraught with peril for most investors. Even the professionals get it wrong, so the smart managers simply work on reducing risk on the downside, or, as Warren Buffett said, "The first rule in investing is don't lose money, the second rule is don't forget rule #1." It's not a revelation to say that Buffett is Brown's hero, a posture of adoration held by most money managers.

"An all-weather fund has upside potential with a downside cushion," Chris Brown says. "It's for people who don't want to make an asset allocation decision. How much risk are you willing to take to achieve a certain return? We strive to offer a good return with reduced risk."

Brown tempers the fund's risk on the bond side by investing in bonds with short maturities and *durations*, a measure of how much a bond price could decline if interest rates rise 1 percent. (The shorter the duration, the lower the interest-rate risk.) With a combination of corporate and government-agency bonds, Brown finds bonds with maturities from three years to five years, so the chance of losing money in the bond market is reduced.

On the stock side, Brown employs a time-tested method of fishing for stocks generally called "growth at a reasonable price," or

GARP (apologies to John Irving). This method involves finding stocks that are growing their profits, yet may be undervalued relative to the market and similar stocks. GARP is a fairly popular way of scouting cheap stocks and employs the best of *value* and *growth* techniques (more on that in chapters 4 and 5). Like stocks and bonds, the value and growth schools are in constant competition. In booming markets, investors tend to chase earnings and favor growth, which has been the case from 1982 through 2000. When the market changes course, the better stock pickers evaluate value, which stresses finding bargains relative to similar companies. As discussed in chapter 1, value managers are bargain pickers, hoping to find companies that are not priced fairly. That means their prices don't reflect the underlying value of all of the company's assets or *book* value.

Sectors and Themes: How Managers Think

Brown's method of picking securities allows him to straddle the vagaries of stock and bond pricing. He doesn't necessarily have to be right with a handful of picks, he just doesn't want to be wrong and get stuck with a stock or bond that loses a third of its value overnight. His value orientation told him that technology stocks were overvalued in August and September 2000, so he reduced his holding of tech stocks from 11 percent to, eventually, 5 percent. Fortunately, he got out of one of the most overvalued sectors in a bubbling market—at about the right time.

Brown is free to move around different *sectors* in the stock market. A sector is a group of companies in more or less the same industry. For example, companies that explore and refine petroleum or methane products are considered to be in the energy sector; companies that develop medical treatments based on genetics are in the biotechnology sector. Wal-Mart and Kmart are blue chips in the retail sector. Sectors march to the beat of their own drummers. Retail sectors move based on consumer spending. Energy companies are hostage to oil and gas prices. All sectors are driven by profits, which is the propeller behind stock prices.

Always striving to find companies that will grow their earnings—and boost their stock price—Brown searches for what money managers call "themes." Unlike the theme papers you wrote in high school, a manager sees a theme as an idea that may push up a stock price. For example, Brown was prescient to realize that there was a burgeoning market for middlemen in the energy business, so he bought Enron, a leading company in the energy trading business. Brown and his analysts concluded that energy prices were heading up, Enron was in the right place at the right time, and they seized upon the theme as a chance to make a profit in the company. Managers typically have target prices at which they think companies will become overvalued relative to the market and they sell. If you go to the supermarket, for example, you know that you're not going to pay $5 for a pound of bananas, but you will buy them if they are $1 or less. Having bought Enron at a decent price, Brown then turned around and sold shares in the company at a profit, which was passed along to Pax World Balanced shareholders in the form of capital gains or reinvested in new shares (if they so chose). Fortunately, Brown was able to sell 70 percent of Pax World's position in Enron long before negative news caused the stock to plummet.

Another safeguard built into Pax World's investment guidelines is that it can't hold more than 5 percent of its portfolio in any one stock. If a company's market value pushes it above the 5 percent limit, Brown will monitor the stock and decide if it *overweights* the portfolio and may sell it. This avoids concentrating too much of the fund's assets in one stock and maintains diversification.

Because Pax World is an SRI fund, there's another level of analysis that its shareholders demand. The company's practices must be screened for employment discrimination, environmental records, and investments in defense, tobacco, and gambling. Brown says his analysts look for "patterns of lawsuits, EPA fines, employment discrimination. All of these issues can impact the company's bottom line. If they treat their employees and the environment well, they are generally more efficient and it adds value to the financial process. This requires research and work to follow through on the screens and it can be challenging."

Brown's holistic approach has made Pax World one of the leaders among balanced funds. It beat the S&P 500 Index by 14.8 percent in 2000 and over the past five years has returned an average 11.76 percent. It achieved these returns with one of the lowest risk ratings from Morningstar. The fund's ability to continue this performance depends on market conditions; however, Brown will consistently maintain the balance between stocks and bonds and temper risk by looking for bargains that have the potential to grow.

Maintaining a Mix of Stocks and Bonds

In addition to its social investing perspective, Pax World Balanced fund embodies one of the rules laid out by legendary investor and teacher Benjamin Graham: "My basic rule is that investors always have a minimum of 25% in bonds or bond equivalents, and a minimum of 25% in common stocks." Graham's dictum is a start for any investor concerned about reducing risk and profiting in a bear market, one that we'll explore further in the next chapter.

Graham, the mentor to Warren Buffett and the "value school" of investing, keyed one of the basic principles of diversification, which requires that you be in a variety of assets that don't move in unison. Graham's principle of diversification was further refined in 1950 by Harry Markowitz, who established some mathematical guidelines for diversification while writing a doctoral dissertation at the University of Chicago. (Along with William Sharpe and Merton Miller, he was awarded the Nobel Prize for his insights.)

The writings of Philip Fisher also influenced generations of investors. Fisher focused less on a company's financial reports and more on the quality of management. As Robert G. Hagstrom Jr., author of several fine books on the value school of investing, explains, "Fisher was aware that superior companies not only possess above-average business characteristics but, equally important, are directed by people with above-average management capabilities."

Graham quite simply became the godfather of a school of investing that is going strong today and will be examined in detail in the next two chapters.

BEST BALANCED FUNDS FOR THE LONG TERM

Fund	5-year Return	Phone
Pax World Balanced Fund	11.76%	(800) 767-1729
Dodge & Cox Balanced Fund	12.60%	(800) 621-3979
Vanguard STAR Fund	9.90%	(800) 662-7447

Returns (annualized) through 12/31/01. *Source:* Morningstar.

Speaking of Balance: What about Real Estate?

While we're on the subject of balance and balancing *your* funds, let's harken back to the Greek concept of *oikos*, the household. In an age obsessed with stocks and bonds, an often-ignored aspect of investing involves real estate. Compared to stocks, the difficult category of real estate (residential real estate in particular) is a tough bird to track. There are more factors influencing local real estate than impact the stock market. So comparing your home to stocks as an asset is really an apples and oranges dilemma. Nevertheless, real estate deserves consideration as part of your portfolio and is a definite component of your net worth (your total assets minus your liabilities).

Real estate's value in a portfolio lies in the fact that it's *not* a stock or a bond and doesn't move in lockstep with those markets. In the words of portfolio managers, it has little *covariance*, meaning its returns don't move in the same direction as stocks or bonds. Harry Markowitz discovered that one of the cornerstones of a diversified portfolio—at least one that balanced risk and return—was that it effectively mixed different *asset classes*. Within stocks and bonds, there are several asset classes by style and capitalization, as we've discussed. There are also nonfinancial classes, like precious metals, coins, collectibles, paintings, antique furniture, and real estate. Since the non–real estate classes are extremely difficult to value (except for precious metals, which are traded on international markets), we'll focus on real estate as something you can value and use to buffer risk in stocks and bonds.

Since there's always a market for real estate—it can be priced, brokered, bought, and sold—it's something that holds value and two parties can generally agree on what it's worth. Within real estate, for example, there's residential (single-family homes, condos), rental residential (apartments), retail (shopping centers, malls), commercial (warehouses), health care (hospitals, nursing homes), and industrial (factories and large facilities). Real estate has its own set of risks and variables that make it different from financial assets, which are priced according to profits and interest rates. Here are some unique characteristics of real estate:

- It can't be moved. Unlike a dollar bill, bond, or stock certificate, you can't hand it to somebody, so its price depends upon where it is. That means it's subject to the market's perception of the local economy. If a warehouse or home is located in a town where businesses are moving out, then the property will become devalued.

- It can be financed. Interest rates make the cost of ownership higher or lower. A lower cost of financing (lower mortgage rate) is generally positive for residential real estate because more people can buy homes, thus driving up demand—and prices.

- It can be turned into a security. Home mortgages are sold to a "secondary market," where they become like stocks and bonds and are bought and sold by investors. This is what Ginnie Mae (GNMA) funds invest in. Investors buy mortgages because they promise a fairly steady income over time.

- It is subject to the laws of supply and demand. If the local economy is strong, and the pace of construction can't keep up with demand, that will force up prices for existing structures. The opposite occurs when the market is glutted or the local economy takes a dive.

WHAT HOLDS UP? WINNING INVESTMENTS DURING THE WORST OF A BEAR MARKET

Investment	Return*
Real estate	9.0%
Intermediate government bonds	5.6%
Money-market funds	4.9%
Balanced funds	3.1%

*3-year annualized return from 9/10/01 through 9/19/01, which reflects the second-worst weekly decline to date in the history of Wall Street. *Source:* Lipper.

Your Home as an Investment?

The argument has been raging for some time that at least when it comes to your home, you should *never* consider it as an investment. After all, do stocks and bonds need painting, new appliances, and gutters? Can you live in your stock portfolio? The structure you live in will always be a depreciating asset. The land, however, is not, since your home occupies a space that usually isn't built on again, which reduces the supply of real estate—and often drives up prices in areas of steady demand.

My unique view on residential real estate is that a home is like a bond. In most places it will pay you the rate of inflation, which is roughly equal to a T-bill return. Then it will pay you a premium or discount based on the health of your local economy. Unless you refinance or hold an adjustable-rate mortgage, your mortgage provides a fixed rate of return for an investor on the secondary market. You don't directly benefit from that, but you can assume that in most places the value in your home pays you an *imputed* return. That means that there's an unstated, invisible appreciation based on the local economy, the type of home you have, supply and demand, and interest rates. And if you rent out your house (or other properties), you have a fairly reliable income stream. At closing time, you see how much appreciation has accumulated once you subtract closing costs, lawyers' fees, taxes, and the agent's commission. By the way, there's also the benefit of writing off your mortgage interest, some of your financing points, and your property taxes, so the *after-tax costs* of owning this asset are partially subsidized by Uncle Sam.

Traditionally, Americans have seen their homes as the largest part of their nest eggs. All they had to do was sell their family home and move to a smaller, less expensive home to reap the appreciation. Under the current tax laws, if your net gain from a home sale is under $500,000 for joint filers ($250,000 for singles), you get to keep those gains tax free. In an age when stocks and bonds have easily outpaced the returns on residential real estate (in most places), your home *isn't* the primary generator of wealth it was in decades past. It's estimated that during the past twenty-five years, home prices have risen 5.8 percent annually, compared with 10.6 percent for the Standard & Poor's 500 Index, according to the Federal National Mortgage Association (Fannie Mae). Your home, however, has a far more intangible value. You can live in the house and benefit from the surrounding community. A stock or bond makes for a poor habitat.

Home prices almost never move in the same direction as the stock market. The one exception used to be high-end real estate in the New York City metropolitan area, but that economy has become much more diverse in the past twenty years, and that's not entirely true today. So your home buffers your exposure in the stock and bond markets. Is it something you should invest in by adding to principal every month? If you have a need to pay off your mortgage early and gain the extra cash flow—say you'll have two kids in college and don't want a mortgage payment when they matriculate—then that's a viable option. Since you are using other people's money to gain a rate of return equal to the rate of inflation—about 3 percent in 2001—it's not, however, the wisest use of your money to pay off your mortgage and certainly not the best investment in the world.

But What about Hot Real Estate Markets?

Because Main Street doesn't care what Wall Street is doing most of the time, you can certainly *consider* real estate as an investment. (Note my emphasis.) Buying homes or apartments—particularly "fixer-uppers" or bargains in a robust or steady market—can be a way to invest. Local real estate, in Markowitz's view, has little "covariance" with the securities markets, so it can offer you diversification and lower the overall risk of your portfolio of assets. Here's a sampling of how much variation there can be in the growth of local real estate. Keep in mind that this is just a snapshot in time and real estate and, like any market, can change quickly in a short period of time.

Like financial markets, real estate markets can also decline over time. However you view real estate—especially if you regard it like a bond—the return is not guaranteed. At worst, you'll probably keep pace with inflation, but it's not like a Treasury bond. The government won't come to your rescue if you *don't* get a 3 percent return per year. The lion's share of real estate investment risk is connected to the local economy, and you'll benefit from some background research on where residential values are headed, especially before you make serious investments in property outside of your home. And if you are considering relocating, look for markets that are desirable, affordable, and not on the ascent. You may find some bargains relative to your market.

Even More Real Estate Diversification:
REITs and Real Estate Funds

Another way to invest in real estate and lower your portfolio risk is to include real estate investment trusts (REITs) or real-estate mutual funds that invest in REITs in your portfolio. REITs invest primarily in commercial, industrial, and apartment properties and pooled assets. You can think of REITs as stocks that only invest in real estate; they are listed and traded on major exchanges. They differ from stocks in that they by law *must* pay investors 90 percent of their returns, which are generated by rents and sales.

HOME PRICES: A SNAPSHOT

Market	Growth	Median Price (in thousands)
Rising Existing Home Prices: A Sampling		
Sacramento, Calif.	23.9%	$176.0
Washington, D.C./Md./Va.	18.6%	$206.7
Charleston, W.V.	15.9%	$110.1
Riverside, Calif.	15.4%	$157.5
Jacksonville, Fla.	13.7%	$111.9
Falling Home Prices		
Melbourne, Fla.	−5.3%	$ 97.4
Gainesville, Fla.	−2.9%	$119.7
Honolulu, Hawaii	−2.1%	$295.0
Portland, Ore.	−0.8%	$171.8
Albuquerque, N.M.	−0.3%	$132.3

This is just a sampling of a point in time and may or may not reflect long-term trends in real estate. *Source:* National Association of Realtors, second quarter, 2001.

REITs offer a useful vehicle to invest in a variety of real estate across the world. Properties range from health-care facilities to apartment buildings, from storage facilities to warehouses. Although REITs are subject to supply and demand and other market forces, they offer a route to diversification not offered by stocks and bonds because they are not moving in sync with those markets. That's Markowitz's covariance factor again, the friend of any risk-reducing investor.

REITS MOVE IN DIFFERENT DIRECTIONS THAN STOCKS

The National Association of Real Estate Investment Trusts (NAREIT), the trade association representing REITs, wanted to know how closely REIT prices followed stock prices over time, so they asked Ibbotson Associates to look at different time periods. The NAREIT study showed that REIT prices declined to 0.25 correlation between large stocks (the S&P 500) and REITs over the past 30 years. That means that 75% of the time REIT prices didn't follow the S&P 500's movement. Virtually the same relationship was seen for small stocks.

In addition to offering diversification, REITs can provide income and enhance return. A NAREIT study showed that a portfolio with 40 percent stocks, 30 percent bonds, 20 percent REITs, and 10 percent U.S. Treasury bills posted an average return of 12.2 percent compared to a portfolio containing 50 percent stocks, 40 percent bonds, and 10 percent T-bills, which returned 11.3 percent (between 1972 and 2000). And with average REIT yields hovering near 7 percent at the end of 2001, REITs are a worthy companion to bonds in any portfolio.

Real-estate mutual funds go one step further by investing in a variety of REITs, which often specialize in specific types of properties, so you can obtain yet another level of diversification and safety beyond that offered by owning a handful of REITs. There are sixty-three mutual funds investing in REITs and they give investors a breadbasket of properties in one package. The Vanguard REIT Index, for example, buys a representative sampling of REITs and manages them relatively inexpensively. Like most REIT funds, this fund handily beat the stock market in 2000, posting a 22.75 percent return.

REITs have had their down years, most notably in 1998 and 1999, when an oversupply of commercial properties depressed prices. In those years, average REIT shares sank 18.8 percent and

6.5 percent respectively, according to NAREIT. REITs can be as volatile or more volatile than stocks. REITs that specialize in the most vulnerable sectors—hotels, commercial or retail properties— have incredible volatility. Hotel REITs, for example, were down a stunning 49 percent at one point in 1998. It makes sense to diversify by owning a number of different kinds of REITs or investing in a real-estate mutual fund that owns a variety of the vehicles. REITs or real-estate mutual funds are good investments for core holdings in your portfolio (say, 10 percent of your total assets), not just in bear markets.

Like your home's value, however, REIT yields are *not* guaranteed and will rise and fall with market conditions. Since you get the greatest amount of diversification through a real-estate mutual fund, the following funds are worth considering:

TOP REAL ESTATE MUTUAL FUNDS

Fund	5-year Return	Phone
Columbia Real Estate	8.31%	(800) 547-7786
Fidelity Real Estate	7.05%	(800) 544-8888
Vanguard REIT Index	7.61%	(800) 662-7447

Returns through 12/31/01. *Source:* Morningstar.

The Only Course: A Balanced Portfolio

You never know which kind of asset is going to perform well and over what period of time. Since few, if any, among us have the ability to predict markets, diversification through a balanced approach is the only holistic defense against the bear and the only way to keep the bull grazing in the pasture. That reminds me of a story involving bulls and President Calvin "Silent Cal" Coolidge, whose one memorable utterance in the 1920s was "The business of America is business."

Coolidge's sharp intellect also produced such statements as "The country is not in good condition," which he observed in

1931 as Herbert Hoover was desperately trying to pull America out of the Great Depression. He followed up that insight with the trenchant observation, "When a great many people are unable to find work, unemployment results."

Coolidge was hoping to apply his keen mind to the problem of the Depression during a visit to the White House in 1931. Hoover had just announced measures designed to revive the devastated economy and was becoming frustrated because he wasn't seeing any results. Coolidge offered this reassurance: "You can't expect to see calves running in the fields the day after you put the bulls to the cows."

"No," replied a beleaguered Hoover, "but I would expect to see some *contented* cows."

I can't offer you contentment as our journey continues; however, I can show you how different kinds of cows can become bulls in any market.

CHAPTER 4

Bargains and Income: Stocks and Bonds That Stand Up during the Storm

Every investor should be prepared financially and psychologically for the possibility of poor short-term results. For example, in the 1973–74 decline, the investor would have lost money on paper, but, if he'd held on and stuck with the approach, he would have recouped in 1975–1976 and gotten his 15% average return for the five-year period.

—Benjamin Graham

Clyde McGregor is built like a football lineman, and possesses the intellect of a college professor. An occasional golf and tennis player, he used to play basketball, but I wouldn't want him setting a pick against me. With Edward Studzinski, he has managed the Oakmark Equity & Income Fund to generate income while preserving and growing capital. Studzinski came on board in 2000, but McGregor has been running the fund since 1995. Like the Pax World Balanced Fund, Oakmark Equity & Income has at least 25 percent of its holdings in bonds; however, the fund parts company with Pax in its approach. As stalwarts in the fine Oakmark team, McGregor and Studzinski run what the industry calls a "value shop." They are bargain hunters first and foremost and will do endless amounts of research to find their bargains.

It's hard to classify McGregor's fund since it does so many things well. It is simultaneously generating income, producing growth, and keeping volatility down. McGregor's team isn't much interested in where the economy is headed, the hottest sector, or even the latest technology. They swim on the bottom of the ocean and see what's floating down, hoping that it will rise again. Fund-rating services are hard-pressed to put a label on the fund. Morningstar calls the fund a "hybrid" or "large-blend" fund, which tells investors nothing about what the fund does or how it performs. The more traditional label is "equity-income," a slightly better description that tells investors it splits its portfolio roughly between 75 percent stocks and 25 percent bonds, but not always. Oakmark provides a somewhat better description: "The fund invests for high current income and preservation and growth of capital. It is designed for investors who want the growth potential of stocks, and the cushion [that] bonds may provide."

Whatever label is attached to Oakmark, it is definitely less risky than a 100 percent stock fund and often features market-beating returns. Although this label is somewhat fudgy as well, Oakmark takes an *eclectic* approach, meaning it achieves lower risk through novel means. Its bond portfolio, for example, contains several high-yield corporate bonds, the bad boys of the bond world that carry the highest risk in return for almost double-digit yields. Where it counts, Oakmark is ahead of the pack, producing a five-year average return of 16.4 percent a year, handily beating its peer-group (of large-blend funds) average of 13.7 percent. The fund has been in the top 10 percent of its class over the last three- to five-year periods.

On the stock side, Oakmark's "deep-value" approach keeps McGregor looking for bargains that no other fund would touch. He finds unlikely picks like J. C. Penney, the musty, old-line department store that was a huge winner for the fund, up 90 percent at one point. Unlike the Pax funds, McGregor doesn't care what a company looks like to other investors; he's buying for price and income. He holds UST, the holding company of U.S. Tobacco, a leading maker of chewing tobacco, which also pays a healthy dividend.

It's also not important to McGregor how big a company is in terms of market capitalization or what industry it represents. Like most deep-value managers, it's the price of a stock—and its capacity to turn around—that interests him. Every value manager makes a bet that they can find a pearl among swine, a gem of a company that the market has underpriced for one reason or another. They are intelligently sneaking around a market maxim that holds that all securities are priced correctly because all the facts about the company are known to the public and market analysts. This is the "efficient market theory."

Value managers like McGregor are betting they can spot stocks that are flying under the radar of market efficiency, take large stakes in them, and hope that the market will realize—and raise—the market value of the company in question. It's like finding a Picasso at a garage sale. The best value managers can do this consistently because they have a team of bloodhounds—their analysts—who are constantly looking for companies that are bruised, beaten, and neglected. Once they get the scent, managers like McGregor can pounce. He places his bets on a few companies that he thinks will see double-digit turnarounds once the market turns his (and the company's, for that matter) way. In the short term, this is a risky strategy if the bets don't pay off. The risk lessens, however, over several years, since value managers like McGregor are not looking for—or expecting—a quick profit.

Case in point is McGregor's purchase of J. C. Penney. When most people think of leading retailers, they think of Wal-Mart, Target, Costco, and Amazon.com. Penney, to most people, hails from another era, when department stores meant clothing on the first floor, appliances on the second, and bargains in the basement. It was the world that Sears dominated for decades. It was a formula that worked before deep-discount, specialty, warehouse retailing, and the Internet sold everything that Penney sold—only cheaper and faster. Penney was a dinosaur, and Wall Street was waiting for changing retail tastes to finally put it out of its misery.

Like any astute value manager, McGregor sensed Penney wasn't getting a fair hearing on Wall Street and listened to what management had to say. "Penney's CEO lays out a plan to earn $5 a share in 2000 and mentions plans for Eckerd [the nation's third-largest drug store chain, which Penney bought]. Eckerd had this idea that they wanted to make it convenient for their customers to get in and out in seven minutes, so they put their prescription counters in the front of the store. Then they figured out, like their main competition, Walgreen's—which has their prescription counter in the back of the store—to move *their* prescription counters to the back. Sales go up. They cut their dividend to two percent and some year-end tax-loss selling makes the stock even more attractive. We figure they've already been through the wringer and it's hard for them to disappoint investors at $25 a share. Later we sell at $50."

McGregor's analysis hinges on value-investing orthodoxy: What is a business really worth and does the stock price reflect its worth or *intrinsic* value? By adding up all of the company's assets and subtracting liabilities—that is, finding its *book* value—value guys like McGregor try to establish a *price-to-book ratio* (p/b ratio). This is the company's stock-market price divided by its per-share book value. You don't need to do the math here, but a p/b ratio of more than 1.0 usually shows that the price of the stock is valued above the total value of the company's assets. In other words, investors attach a premium to a high p/b ratio company, which means it's no bargain.

Value investors first determine if a stock is a bargain by looking at the company's net worth, rather than focusing on earnings growth, which is a secondary concern. Growth-oriented investors, in contrast, first look at *price/earnings ratios* or p/e ratios. The p/e is calculated by dividing the current stock price by the last twelve months of earnings per share. This ratio tells investors how much the market is willing to pay for a dollar's worth of profits. The higher the p/e, the greater value the market places on those earnings.

Neither p/b nor p/e ratios tell the whole story of why value players like McGregor can outfox the market at times. Like the constant tug-of-war between stocks and bonds, growth and value are constantly wrestling each other for dominance in the stock (and sometimes) bond markets. When earnings are consistent and upsurging—as they were between 1991 and 1999—growth carries the day and value is out of favor. When earnings across the board fall out of favor, as in bearish markets, value is the more dependable way of making money, which is why funds like Oakmark are worth considering.

Value and Growth: The Road to Risk

A few months after I visited Clyde McGregor, the *Wall Street Journal*, in headier times "The Diary of the American Dream," ran a story headlined "NASDAQ Companies Losses Erase 5 Years of Profit." I'm not quite sure why this piece ran on page C3 instead of on the front page, but its conclusions were shocking. Losses from the top technology companies in the NASDAQ eliminated all of the profits from the stock run-up of the 1990s. In late 2001, the darlings of the info age, the monsters of "ego space," were in tatters. Intel, Microsoft, Oracle, Dell, and Cisco Systems were still in the black, but JDS Uniphase, VeriSign, and CMGI were laid to waste. JDS Uniphase's losses alone were $51.6 billion as of 2001. The Internet darling Excite@Home lost $10 billion. These were companies that investors could not buy enough of at the beginning of 2000. The *Journal* estimated that the collective losses of the NASDAQ leaders chewed up five years' worth of profits. The all-electronic market was back where it started in 1995.

If earnings disappear, what's left? Can you make money with companies that produce no profit? Well, for one thing, unprofitability makes a company an unlikely candidate for short-term growth in its market price (in normal times). More important, it makes companies that had earnings all along and were underpriced relative to fad stocks even more valuable. Enter our mattress-loving friends in the value kingdom.

BEAR-BEATERS: STOCKS THAT SOARED
IN THE SEPTEMBER 2001 ROUT

Company	Increase*
Northrop Grumman	15.9%
Lockheed Martin	14.8%
General Dynamics	9.2%
Placer Dome	5.7%
Washington Mutual	5.5%
Golden Western	5.5%
Newmont Mining	5.2%
Barrick Gold	3.5%
Countrywide Credit	3.1%
Fannie Mae	2.8%

*Returns reflect the period from September 10 through September 18. The top three stocks benefited from the perception of increased military spending; Placer Dome, Newmont, and Barrick are gold-mining stocks that spurt in times of worldwide crisis or inflation, but have been awful investments long term; Washington Mutual, Golden Western, Countrywide Credit, and Fannie Mae deal in mortgages. Interest rates dropped after September 11. *Source:* Reuters and the *Wall Street Journal.*

Size Matters, Sometimes

Before I outline more of the value school's philosophy, I need to explain a little more about capitalization, which is not as important to value investors as finding an outright bargain. Knowing a little about capitalization, however, will tell you something about risk. Capitalization, you will recall, is the market price of a stock multiplied by its outstanding shares. With any public company, it's an easy calculation to make, and generally gives a thumbnail sketch of how much investors value a company. In recent times, sales and profits were used to rank companies in lists like the Fortune 500 and Forbes 400. Now it's market size that matters.

Market capitalization doesn't really tell you much about how a company is run, but it does tell you the plurality opinion on how much the market thinks a company is worth. The greatest amount of attention—in the market and the press and among active investors—is paid to the large-capitalization or "big-cap" stocks. These are the GEs and Microsofts of the world. Every drop of perspiration of every major big-cap executive is studied carefully to see which way earnings will go. The big boys account for some 72.5 percent of the dollar value of all stocks listed, according to Ibbotson, so maybe that's why they garner so much attention.

The next tier—stocks with market caps between approximately $1 billion and $10 billion—are called "mid-cap" stocks. These are lesser-known companies, like National City, which as a whole comprise about 11 percent of the market. The rest of the more than six thousand listed stocks comprise less than 17 percent of the market and fall into vaguely defined categories called "small-caps" or "micro-caps." A loose definition of a small cap is any company with a market capitalization of $1 billion or below, but there are always arguments in the industry as to where the line should be drawn.

Market cap is important to value managers because the lower you get on the market-cap totem pole, the lower the likelihood that Wall Street is paying attention—and the greater chance of finding unique information about a company and plucking a bargain. I don't think any one hundred Americans could easily name a single mid- or small-cap stock, while most of us can easily come up with big caps like General Motors, Procter & Gamble, and Coca-Cola.

Mid- and small-sized companies don't always move in the shadow of the big boys. They may tag along because they are just getting started, not well known to the investing public, and have lower profiles, so not as many Wall Street analysts or mutual-fund managers follow them. Ultimately, that means that there's less of an onus on the mid and small caps to post consistently higher earnings. The Street isn't hanging on to every hint of an earnings "surprise," so they tend to be less volatile.

Capitalization also comes into play because smaller companies tend to be more nimble; they can move in and out of businesses more efficiently, they need less capital to grow their enterprises, and their mistakes are less publicized. So they tend to have much more promising upsides and their downsides are not as steep as their big-cap brothers. And that's why value managers often gravitate to the mid and small caps when the big boys are overpriced or are just not performing well. Managers like McGregor stick with big caps, although capitalization is less important than the price and appreciation potential of the company.

Capitalization plus Style a Better Guide to Performance

Being a value investor means taking lower risk, but you can enhance your returns in down markets by also looking at the capitalization of the companies in your portfolio. Since value investors are more concerned with the long-term worth of a company, in the short term they are not obsessed with returns and can be more patient in waiting for smaller-cap companies to produce earnings. Looking at historical returns of investments is always a dangerous business anyway. It's misleading to think that performance over a long period of time will tell you anything about the present or future.

Although long-term small-cap stocks outperform large caps as a class, there's much more to the story. Investment style also enters into the picture. Use real estate as an example. Let's say there are two investors, Joe and Jerry. Joe buys all of his real estate at a 30 percent discount to listed price. He insists on that discount or he doesn't buy the property. Jerry, on the other hand, believes the properties he buys are all fairly and efficiently priced and he is even willing to pay a premium, because he knows appreciation is virtually guaranteed. Which investor comes out ahead in the long run? By picking up bargains, Joe is looking at better profit margins than Jerry, all other things being equal. As the table below shows, when the bear market hit in March of 2001, small and bargain-priced stocks did the best, while small, overpriced stocks got hit the worst.

HOW VALUE INVESTORS FARED BY STYLE
IN THE EARLY BEAR MARKET

Capitalization/Style	Return*
Large value	9%
Mid-cap value	28%
Small-cap value	20%
Large growth	−33%
Mid-cap growth	−45%
Small growth	−46%

*Returns from 2/28/00 to 3/31/01. *Source:* Kanon Bloch Carré, www.kanon.com.

It pays to shop for bargains when times are tough. Investors who buy stocks (or bonds, for that matter) at a discount to market value do better over time than those who pay the going rate for a security. This idea not only sounds appealing, but is backed up by a solid body of academic research. In a famous 1993 paper entitled "Contrarian Investment, Extrapolation and Risk," Professors Josef Lakonishok, Andre Shleifer, and Robert Vishny found that "value" stocks purchased at a discount outperform stocks that are more highly valued over time.

The hidden gem in the "contrarian" strategy is that value stocks also did well during the stock market's worst twenty-five months from April 30, 1968, through April 20, 1990 (the period of the study). Having a basket of low-priced stocks, you can conclude from the study, is more profitable than buying stocks "at retail." The cherry picking of cheap stocks also implies that you need to ignore the companies that the market values most highly—those stocks with sterling earnings reports. Value managers like Mc-Gregor look beyond the few warts on the frog to find the inner prince.

Like Graham and Buffett, Phil Fisher also believed that superior companies are often overlooked. These companies have bad years, but over the decades they prevail. As Robert G. Hagstrom Jr. said of Fisher, "The characteristic of a business that most impressed

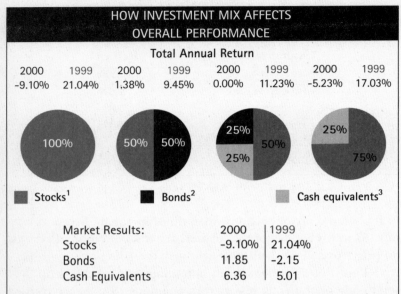

HOW INVESTMENT MIX AFFECTS OVERALL PERFORMANCE

Total Annual Return

2000	1999	2000	1999	2000	1999	2000	1999
-9.10%	21.04%	1.38%	9.45%	0.00%	11.23%	-5.23%	17.03%

■ Stocks[1]   ■ Bonds[2]   ■ Cash equivalents[3]

Market Results:	2000	1999
Stocks	-9.10%	21.04%
Bonds	11.85	-2.15
Cash Equivalents	6.36	5.01

These indexes are not available for direct investment. Measured by: [1]S&P 500 Stock Index, an unmanaged index of stocks of 500 major corporations; [2]Lehman Brothers Government/Corporate Bond Index, an unmanaged index of investment grade corporate and government bonds with maturities of one year or more; and, [3]Merrill Lynch 3-Month T-Bill Index, an unmanaged index that measures returns of three-month U.S. Treasury Bills.

Sources: Russell Data Services and Newkirk Products, Inc.

Fisher was a company's ability to grow sales and profits over the years at rates greater than the industry average."

One of the best value fund managers of all time, John Templeton, was a staunch value investor. His Templeton Growth Fund was the best-performing mutual fund from 1964 to 1994. Although Templeton has since retired from managing money, his techniques are shared by a whole group of managers who now follow Warren Buffett's every move. Templeton, who employed value techniques on stocks all over the world, did well because he was often a contrarian, buying inexpensive stocks that were out of favor. McGregor followed the same path in buying J. C. Penney and a host of other neglected companies.

As Templeton's record and subsequent studies proved, the value technique works in finding winners in the United States as well as abroad. A 1991 Morgan Stanley study of 2,349 companies found that the bargain approach even worked with a "world" portfolio of 80 percent non-U.S. companies. The average return of the value stocks from 1981 to 1990 was compared to the benchmark Morgan Stanley Capital International global equity index. If you had $1 million to invest in these low-priced stocks starting in 1981, it would have increased to $7,953,000 at the end of 1991, compared to $3,651,000 from more expensively priced stocks. Price does matter to the value camp and it's more profitable over time.

What about periods in which the core of the U.S. stock market is getting sold off? Let's assume the thrill is gone and investors are heading for the exits on all of the big-cap stocks. In this case, the value approach still holds up. In a study by Kanon Bloch Carré, they found that large value outperformed large-growth stocks by 42 percentage points in the last thirteen months of the bull market that ultimately ended (by their definition) on March 31, 2001. Style matters if you're in a pinch.

To find an even fluffier cushion when the market gets rocked, a fund that combines a value approach with bonds and income-paying stocks is a good investment. You probably won't outperform the market with an equity-income fund in good times, but you will have some padding if things turn nasty. Keep in mind that the best-managed companies over the long run have relatively low debt, own shares in their own company, are not capital intensive, are not subject to extensive government regulation, are reducing costs constantly, and are often out of favor, according to portfolio manager Charles Brandes. Of course, these are just starting points for a whole course on value investing, which I will cover in greater detail in the next chapter.

TOP-QUALITY EQUITY-INCOME FUNDS

Fund	5-year Return	Phone
Oakmark Equity and Income	16.39%	(800) 625-6275
T. Rowe Price Equity-Income	10.46%	(800) 638-5660
Fidelity Equity-Income II	9.99%	(800) 544-8888

Returns through 12/31/01. *Source:* Morningstar.

Where You Find Balance

To understand the ultrarational world of value investing, you need to take a walk in what Warren Buffett calls "Graham and Doddsville." That means studying the Rosetta stone of value investing, *Graham and Dodd's Security Analysis*, the 1934 classic. This is Benjamin Graham's legacy and the starting point for any aspiring value investor. Although you may find most of this tome impenetrable, I found one section that resounds with clarity and purpose:

> The common goal of all investors is to acquire assets that are at least fairly priced and preferably underpriced. Should such assets become overvalued, the investors' goal is to recognize the fact and dispose of them. Since this valuation relates to unknown future events, its accuracy may depend as much on the economic, capital market, sector and industry factors at work as on specific company performance.

The proof, for value investors, is in the "fairness" of the pricing (read "priced cheaply relative to the competition"), which they hope leads to performance in lean times as well as fat times. Everything else is a "top-down" consideration, that is, a focus on external events like economic reports, stock market averages, and whether an industry is in or out of favor.

There is a familiar fable that describes investment philosophies indirectly: "The Princess and the Pea." Remember the Hans Christian Andersen tale of the would-be princess who is tested by a prince, who is unsure she is a real princess? He stacks twenty mattresses on top of a hidden pea and asks the lass to spend the night on the huge bed. In the morning, she complains of a stiff back because she felt the pea, and only a princess could have such a delicate frame. (If she hadn't felt the pea, she would have been one of the rabble.) In growth investing, the pea is earnings. Without earnings, you have no princesses, and certainly no growth. In value investing, forget about the pea, because you have lots of mattresses. Who cares if the princess is comfortable or not, or even if she's royalty? She can sleep in the Budgetel for all we care.

Value investors like to think that they know that there are several princesses on top of all of those mattresses in the market. It just takes some skill and experience to find them, which you can do, too, if you follow their philosophy with conviction (or just invest in their mutual funds).

CHAPTER 5

Growth plus Value: How to Outsmart the Market

Of the various ways of making money in securities, I know no better way than through a close watch on management. Changes I particularly refer to are those where companies have been in difficulty, their stocks depressed, and general dissatisfaction expressed—and where a new management comes in and invariably begins by sweeping out the accounting cobwebs. . . . Thus an investor at this juncture often gets in at the bottom or the beginning of a new cycle."

—Gerald Loeb

Being a mutual fund manager is a bit like being a wildcat oil driller. You mostly hit dry patches and try to drill where the other guys aren't. When you hit a patch of Texas gold, then you're in business and everyone knows it. In the abstract world of money management, fund managers hit more dry patches than gushers. When they hit petroleum, it makes their year, creating heroes in a world so competitive that everyone takes notice and most fail. To find their fortune, they all read the same sacred texts by Benjamin Graham, Philip Fisher, Philip Carret, and Warren Buffett. They calculate the same equations and talk to the same companies. While focused on *not losing* their clients' money, they try to make a few bets that carry as little downside as they can get. Value managers tend to scour the Permian basin of forgotten, neglected, and unseen companies. They probe balance sheets, talk to customers, drill CEOs. They are constantly seeking a piece of information that will confer upon them the market's blessing: a hidden fact about a profitable business, an undervalued asset, a turn-around strategy from the new guy at the head of the conference table. One bad guess is excusable; even a bad year is okay. Two bad years and they are told to leave a trail of dust.

Bill Miller hasn't seen a bad year since Saddam Hussein was chased out of Kuwait City more than a decade ago. Although his Legg Mason Value Trust fund lost 6.2 percent in 2000 when the S&P 500 lost 9 percent, he's still scoring where it counts—he beat the S&P benchmark average for the tenth consecutive year. No active fund manager can make that claim, which puts him in a league with Buffett and Lynch in the pantheon of money runners. In a world in which beating the S&P just two years in a row is a near-Herculean feat, Miller doesn't have a "master-of-the-universe" kind of attitude. He is as taciturn as a tax preparer and as precise as a neurosurgeon (what he does is often more complicated than brain surgery).

Miller's mind is coiled, ready to pounce. For a man who has been more successful than any of his contemporaries, his heroes are people like William James, the philosopher and psychologist. Like James, Miller explores every quantum bit of knowledge he can find before he makes a decision. Seeking the esthetic of hidden profit, Miller is an archaeologist of the unknown material fact, the tightly wound packet of energy that will send a stock from the black hole of market obscurity to the stellar recognition of a stock the Street wants to own.

Starting in finance as a treasurer for a supplier to steel and cement products companies, Miller didn't come from the right places to do what he's doing. After graduating with honors from Washington and Lee University in 1972, he went overseas as a military intelligence officer. He pursued his doctorate in philosophy at Johns Hopkins, went to J. E. Baker Company as treasurer, and started as a fund analyst at Legg Mason in Baltimore in 1981. Now he's managing $25 billion, but he's as circumspect as a graduate student before a dissertation defense.

Miller's humility is like an aura. He doesn't swagger and openly discusses how he achieves his results. With the discipline of a drill sergeant, the quantitative mind of a physicist, and the daring of a stock-car driver, he races into his method for finding bargain stocks. He goes against the grain a lot of the time. Some of his favorites include Eastman Kodak, Amazon.com, and AOL Time Warner. While these stocks may look sour in the short term, Miller doesn't care. He'll wait a few years to see his stocks rise to the occasion.

"There's no off-season for me," Miller begins. "I invest in companies for a three- to ten-year life span, so that lowers the risk of my portfolio. Risk is calibrated to time horizon."

Paraphrasing Buffett's dictum not to lose money, Miller launches into his controversial decision to buy AOL (now AOL Time Warner) in the fall of 1996 when nobody wanted it and AOL subscribers could barely access the Internet through the on-line service. His purchase was anathema to most of the value orthodoxy: he was buying a high-profile growth company in the technology sector. Only the hot-shot sector-fund guys did that. Value guys bought companies nobody heard of, in places where the Wall Street suits wouldn't soil their Guccis. AOL had been trumpeted on CNBC multiple times, for God's sake. Nevertheless, Miller doesn't think like most fund managers. Growth is actually okay to him, as long as he can get it for a song, a sweet little ditty at that.

At the time of Miller's purchase, AOL's price had collapsed from the 70s to the 20s. It had gone from info age wunderkind to an incompetent, snot-nosed Internet service geek. The Street thought the company was toast because its millions of subscribers had a rough time getting onto the World Wide Web, which was its raison d'être.

"Despite significant log-on problems, AOL's existing customers weren't switching to the Microsoft Network or Compuserve, and its customer base actually continued to grow. When we analyzed traffic patterns of customers using the services, we found one reason why. AOL customers spent eighty percent of their time using its proprietary service rather than the Internet, while customers of the Microsoft Network spent only twenty percent on the proprietary service. The AOL value proposition [the content AOL offered] was clearly very powerful. But we knew people wouldn't stay with AOL if they couldn't log on. So we analyzed how long it would take AOL to solve this problem. Our analysis suggested that AOL could deploy the fix quickly enough and had sufficient capital to do so."

Miller held on to AOL and made huge profits—thirty to forty times the original investment—when the service figured out how to smooth out its Internet connections (only to see it drop 54 percent in value last year). Then Miller further piqued his critics by buying Amazon.com. Like all good value managers, he got into the minds of the executives of the company he owned, saw how they ran their business, discovered how they could work out their problems, and held on while they executed their solution.

His technique was to use the wisdom from all of his predecessors and contemporaries: Peter Lynch, Warren Buffett, John Neff, Mario Gabelli, Chris Davis, and Mason Hawkins. All have fairly secure places in the "value hall of fame," but only Lynch, Buffett, and Neff have made it outside the inner sanctum of the most serious investors.

Miller cites a phrase used by the legendary value investor John Templeton to describe when he knows a stock may be ripe for the picking. "I look at when there are extremes of emotion, or as Templeton said, the 'point of maximum pessimism.' " That meant loading up on AOL and Amazon.com when the Wall Street consensus was that the companies were history. That meant getting into the heads of the managers of those companies to see how they would (and could) work things out. Like Buffett, he concentrates on the unique nature of the franchise he is buying. He's not buying a stock, he's buying the human element of management and its ability to change and transform a losing situation into a winning one.

"I look at the franchise and the history of the business. I look at their industry, the market for their products and if they can sustain the return on capital. I look at the central tendency of valuation."

Now Miller is talking his own, highly refined dialect. His process looks at whether the company he is prospecting is inexpensive relative to its intrinsic value.

> We project cash flows under a variety of scenarios. Each scenario gives us a different value and then we see how those numbers cluster. If they cluster around the same range, then we have a pretty high confidence in that range. Then I talk to management and see whether they can motivate people, if they are making quality products, if they have customer loyalty, common sense, and good relations with the government and employees. Is it a quality company run by quality people?

Miller is, by all accounts, an ace at judging whether a company's management can turn around a bad situation, but he can be wrong, such as the time when he bought computer maker Gateway, another untraditional pick for a value manager.

Even more surprising about Miller is that, despite his reputation as a value manager, he says he "rejects the distinction between growth and value. Growth is an input into the value equation. We are driven by where the best values are."

There's a reason why Miller is on the board of directors of the Santa Fe Institute, where the top minds of the world gather to discuss the cerebral pastiche of nonlinear systems, complexity, and chaos theories. His deep-thinking value approach to growth extends to old-line companies like Kodak and new economy companies like Nokia. He bought Nokia in 1995, for example, when the business was dominated by #1 Motorola and #2 Ericsson. Now Nokia is the cell phone market leader with about a third of the market. He's been guessing right for a long time, having doubled money from a high-school summer job by investing it in RCA in 1965 through 1966.

But Miller also ascribes to the value school's orthodoxy: Own a business at a discount; *invest* rather than trade; buy a business that earns a return higher than its cost of capital (the expenses it incurs to run the company). Miller's approach is not for the weak of heart. Among value managers, he's not known for taking the safe road. His level of analysis is intensive even for a value manager, but his big bets could blow up or simply not produce the results he expects. After all, no amount of research will tell him which way the business cycle or economy is headed—which value managers say isn't relevant (at least that's what they tell their shareholders). Miller's style also defies easy categorization because he combines the growth and value schools so well. Morningstar vaguely defined his style (for the flagship Value Trust Fund) as "large-cap blend," which doesn't tell the story.

Although Miller thinks the S&P will grow in the 6 percent to 8 percent range in coming years (echoing the age of diminished expectations), he turns whimsical when he reflects on his success. "You know how to beat Tiger Woods? Don't play him at golf. You need a competitive advantage or don't compete." And one more wager from the man you wouldn't want to bet against when it comes to the stock market: He thinks Bill Gross's prediction that stocks won't go much higher than a 5 percent annual rate of return is wrong.

Value in a Nutshell: How You Can Find It

To say that the value style of investing is the most successful way to mine the canyons of the stock market is like saying that all you need is a submarine to explore the entire ocean. It's rarely that simple and gets complicated when you explore the details of what the Bill Millers and Warren Buffetts of the world are talking about. You can, of course, save yourself a lot of time and mental exertion by simply buying their funds. You might find Buffett's Berkshire Hathaway a little pricey—and it's like a mutual fund, it's a company that owns other companies outright (but doesn't run them), like Geico Insurance, and large stakes in others, like the Washington Post Company. As I write this in late 2001, Berkshire

Hathaway is trading at $68,000 a share. The Oracle of Omaha (Buffett's moniker) doesn't believe in stock splits. If you want some quality, affordable value mutual funds, skip to the end of this chapter. If you want to know how they evaluate companies, read on.

I want to point out a few salient points, however, about why value investing is such a potent style over time. Value stresses holding stocks for the long term, which, in the short attention span of Wall Street, is often one year. Buffett, in contrast, stresses that his holding period is "forever," although he admits to mistakes now and again. (U.S. Airways is a case in point.) Holding stocks reduces the chance of missing a business cycle or stock rebound because the manager steps away from a hunch that the stock should be trading higher. That translates to less volatility in down markets.

Value investing is also about, in the parlance of baseball, "hitting them where they ain't." Value managers are famous for their belief that most of the market is wrongheaded about particular companies that have hidden virtues that only they can see. "An entire school of investing is based on the premise that over short periods the market is often misguided but over the long run true value will win out," note Gary Belsky and Thomas Gilovich in *Why Smart People Make Big Money Mistakes* (Simon & Schuster, 1998), an informative study of investor psychology. Yes, value investors have a conceit that they know something you don't about companies that are likely to rise in value. No, they are not always right, but when they are, they do very well because they have bought companies that typically have little downside.

More important, it is a fairly solid fact that value investing is far more profitable. When you average all value stocks (large and small), you get an average return of 16.6 percent since 1928, according to Ibbotson, versus 11.7 percent for all growth stocks. Like most of the market, value goes up and down in cycles. When growth is in favor, value is not (see the chart at the top of page 81). But over time, value wins out.

While a 5 percent difference rate of return favoring growth doesn't sound like much, over twenty or thirty years the difference

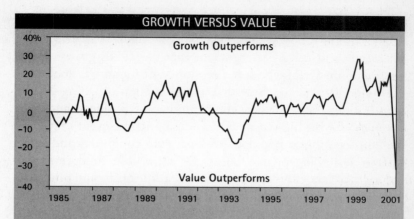

GROWTH VERSUS VALUE

Growth Outperforms

Value Outperforms

This chart compares the performance of growth and value stocks (as represented by the S&P 500/BARRA Value index and the S&P 500/BARRA Growth Index). For years in which the line is above the center of the chart, growth outperformed value; when the line is below the center, value outperformed growth. *Source:* The Vanguard Group.

in the amount of money you would compound is striking. Here's what compounded returns look like at some various rates of return. (Note: This shows only a 3 percent difference.)

VIVE LA DIFFERENCE: VALUE'S ADVANTAGE

$10,000 Invested at . . .

Taxable Account	Tax-Deferred Account
19% for 30 years= $171,743	$760,838
19% for 20 years= $ 66,566	$179,554
19% for 10 years= $ 25,800	$ 42,374
16% for 30 years= $102,820	$353,690
16% for 20 years= $ 47,285	$107,750
16% for 10 years= $ 21,825	$ 32,825

Source: www.cuna.org.

The 1990s a Fluke for Growth?

It's possible to make the argument that the 1990s growth boom was an anomaly. Maybe some economic historian will look back on the 1990s and conclude that a combination of falling interest rates, falling trade barriers, more productive business, and baby boomers chasing big-return stocks was a onetime event that made growth investing so popular. After all, with computers and information technology, large businesses were able to dramatically reduce their labor and operations costs. Trade tariffs and other barriers went away thanks to the North American Free Trade Agreement and the World Trade Organization. And 77 million investors were anxious to save for their retirements, so they chased any positive earnings report or growth-oriented mutual funds they could find. A unique moment in history? Perhaps. Maybe there's another decade or two left to this scenario before the growth party is over. No predictions here.

Or maybe the growth parade really was a fluke and productivity, globalism, and baby boomers have reached a plateau in the grand scheme of things. If you examine every decade going back to the 1920s, the only time growth beat value as a style of investing (other than in the '90s) was in the 1930s, when the bottom kept falling for stocks and there was nothing but growth from the depths of the Depression.

Once again, a dollars-and-cents comparison is in order. From 1927 to 2000, if you had that mythical breadbasket of all large-growth stocks starting with $100, you'd have $932,130 at the end of 2000. With the same amount invested at the same time in all value stocks, you'd have $7,755,390 at the end of the same period.

Value Isn't Always Valuable

Before you get too excited and dump your entire portfolio into value funds, we need to stop for a minute. As you can see, there are times when value investing languishes. It doesn't work all the time, as any value investor can tell you if they had most of their money in value stocks during the 1990s. It may well be that value works worst in a cautious or turbulent market.

The 1930s and 1990s were highly deflationary and ultimately led into more prosperous times. Remember that the 1980s started out with double-digit inflation and interest rates and by the end of the century inflation was running under 3 percent. That's pretty bullish for producing earnings that are not saddled with high costs of doing business. Value reigns supreme when the business cycle is heading south. That's a fairly safe assumption. If profits are going to be lagging due to a slack economy, value is a safer place to be than growth. The downside is not as steep.

My observation is reinforced by research conducted by John Bajkowski of the American Association of Individual Investors, who in researching all of the major styles of investing in the 2000 bear market found: "As a general rule of thumb, approaches that focus on value tend to have less portfolio turnover [buying and selling of stocks] than pure growth approaches, tend to be less volatile, and outperform other approaches during bear markets."

How Does Value Work: The Nuts and Bolts

The language of value investing is quantity and quality. The quality side was summarized by Bill Miller fairly well, and he articulates what nearly every value investor looks for when vetting the management of a company. On the quantity side, there's a little math involved, so if you're satisfied you've learned enough about value investing, skip to the end of the chapter to see my picks for the best value mutual funds.

Value investors are sticklers for details that most investors won't take the time to divine. They are looking for insights on how a company that's underpriced, relative to the market, may become more attractive to the rest of the market. They do this by examining:

- **Price/earnings ratio.** As we mentioned, this percentage is determined by dividing the current stock price by the trailing twelve-month earnings per share. This earnings "multiple" tells investors how much the market values a dollar of earnings. If a stock's p/e is 40, it's trading at forty times earnings. This is a number that should be compared to the average p/e of the industry the stock represents. A low p/e is more attractive to value investors than a high one, particularly one that is below an industry average. Value investors shunned nearly all of the technology stocks of the bull market because of sky-high p/e's, including some as high as 200.

- **Price/book ratio.** The market price of a stock divided by its per-share book value. The book value is to value investors what the bull is to the matador. They zero in on book values because they represent the value of the company's tangible assets. That means accounting for all of the company's operations and assigning a dollar value to it. A p/b ratio under 1.00 means that the price of the stock may not reflect the value of those assets, signaling a possible bargain. The p/b ratio, however, doesn't address the nontangible assets such as franchise value, patents, or trademarks.

- **Sales growth.** Not as important as earnings, but a factor that drives profits. Typically, a company with improving sales growth will boost earnings. In legendary value investor John Neff's view, rising earnings must be supported by rising sales to make the company more appealing.

- **Free cash flow.** This is the amount of money a company has left over once it has paid for capital expenditures. It's preferable to investors for this money to go back into the company to buy equipment or grow its business, pay dividends, or buy back stock, which boosts the stock price.

- **Operating margin.** This is profit that the company uses to run the business. It needs to be compared to similar businesses and its respective industry. Is the company as profitable as the competition? Are its operating margins going up or down?

- **High dividend yields.** This has been a fairly consistent starting point for investors for decades and not just for value players. Companies with low p/e's (and stock prices) often have high dividend yields, a percentage of dividends based on their current stock price. Dividends serve as a buffer against stock prices falling. Even if the stock price tanks, you still have that dividend coming in every quarter, so you have some protection on the downside. Many investors have structured entire portfolios based on dividend-rich companies (see chapter 9), but dividends are only part of the story. Dividends are usually an indication that a company is profitable and willing to share a percentage of its earnings with investors. But they tell no tale about the quality of management.

▪ **Return on equity (ROE).** Of all of the measures used by value investors, this figure is the most elusive and most misunderstood. Fundamentally, this is a ratio that shows how shareholders have benefited by management's investments in the company: profit divided by shareholder equity at the end of the year divided by equity at the beginning of the year divided by 2. In an example offered by the American Association of Individual Investors (AAII), if a company earned $10 million, started the year with $10 million in equity, and finished with $30 million in equity, its ROE would be 40 percent (shareholder's equity is the company's assets minus liabilities, "net worth" to personal investors). If a company produces a higher-than (industry)-average ROE, it's not only growing the business, it's building shareholder wealth as well. ROE is Warren Buffett's most publicized way of tracking consistent managers over the long run; companies need to be able to *sustain* high ROE to make his grade.

Summing Up the Value Approach

I can't presume to do the value approach justice in a few pages. If you are interested in picking stocks using a value regimen, I recommend a number of texts on the subject in the Resources section at the end of this book. There are dozens of other facets to this thoroughly intellectual process.

In studying value investors, you will find that they are inordinately patient and wait for the market to restore their companies to what they believe is a "fair" value. They are the defenders of the downtrodden, but only in the sense that their research is designed to make them profit by the market's lack of vision. Here are a few funds that have vision in spades:

COMPANIES THAT PRODUCED RETURN ON EQUITY GREATER THAN 15% (1989–1999)

Company	ROE (Average)
Coca-Cola	45.6%
American Express	18.2%
Gillette	34.8%
Freddie Mac	18.7%
Wells Fargo	17.6%
Walt Disney	16.0%
Washington Post	15.8%

Not coincidentally, these stocks are all long-term holdings of Warren Buffett's Berkshire Hathaway. *Source:* Timothy Vick, *AAII.*

TOP VALUE MUTUAL FUNDS

Fund	5-year Return	Phone
High to Moderate Risk		
Legg Mason Value	16.87%	(800) 577-8589
T. Rowe Price Capital Appreciation	12.04%	(800) 638-5660
Selected American Shares	12.45%	(800) 279-0279
Low Risk		
Clipper Fund	17.83%	(800) 776-5033
Third Avenue Value	12.55%	(800) 443-1021
Scudder-Dreman High Return Equity A	12.56%	(800) 621-1048

Returns (annualized) through 12/31/01. *Source:* Morningstar.

Value and Patience

I trust that Miller and his cadre of value investors would agree that his school of investing isn't for everyone because it involves a degree of examination, insight, philosophy, and patience that many investors don't have—or don't wish to acquire. It's a combination of these factors—plus a bit of luck—that makes value investing thrive. It's a philosophy built on balance and hope. That reminds me of a passage in Plato's *Republic* written more than twenty-three hundred years ago that still rings true. Socrates is conversing with Adeimantus about money and the discussion leads into the relationship between money and virtue:

> SOCRATES: . . . And then one, seeing another grow rich, seeks to rival him, and thus the great mass of the citizens become lovers of money.
>
> ADEIMANTUS: Likely enough.
>
> S: And so they grow richer and richer, and the more they think of making a fortune the less they think of virtue; for when riches and virtue are placed together in the scales of the balance, the one always rises as the other falls.
>
> A: True.
>
> S: And in proportion, as riches and rich men are honored in the state, virtue and the virtuous are dishonored.
>
> A: Clearly.
>
> S: And what is cultivated, and that which has no honor is neglected.
>
> A: That is obvious.
>
> S: And so at last, instead of loving contention and glory, men become lovers of trade and money; they honor and look up to the rich man, and they make a ruler of him, and dishonor the poor man.
>
> A: They do so.

Socrates goes on to talk about the connection between money and citizenship (he could easily be talking about U.S. campaign financing), but his larger point is that virtue needn't be discarded in a materialistic age. You can be a patient investor and do quite well. After all, patience is a virtue, and it's often rewarded in value investing. Value investing is about finding hidden virtues in a stock—although there are other approaches to consider that flow from the value philosophy.

CHAPTER 6

Finding the Middle Ground: Mid-Cap and Small-Cap Investing

Let us not repine, or so much as think the gifts of God unequally dealt, if we see another abound with riches; when, as God knows, the cares that are the keys that keep those riches, hang often so heavily at the rich man's girdle, that they clog him with weary days, and restless nights, even when others sleep quietly.
—Izaak Walton, *The Compleat Angler*

The name of John W. Rogers Jr.'s money management company speaks elegant couplets about his investing style and approach. Ariel Capital Management manages institutional money and offers several mutual funds, among them the Ariel Fund and Ariel Appreciation Fund, which have performed handsomely in recent years. Readers of the Bard will tell you that Ariel was a sprite imprisoned by Prospero, the exiled magician in *The Tempest*, Shakespeare's last play and perhaps most enigmatic "comedy." The sprite does Prospero's bidding to entrance and entrap the men responsible for Prospero's exile from Milan, who are conveniently shipwrecked on the island in a storm Prospero brews up. As a slave of the island and of Prospero, Ariel floats in and out at the beck and call of Prospero, who eventually sets him free once he has done his magic and Prospero can claim his rightful title in Italy.

Ariel, with $6.2 billion in assets under management, occupies territory that is a netherworld for most of the investing public. It buys and sells companies that are in the mid- to small-capitalization universe, companies whose market value lies between roughly $200 million and $10 billion. Like Warren Buffett, Rogers and his co-chief investment officer, Eric McKissack, hail from the value school. They are experts at plucking bargains from the bin of obscurity and holding them for years until they appreciate in value. The motto of the company, "slow and steady wins the race," refers to Aesop's fable of the tortoise and the hare. Rogers is betting on the tortoise.

Ariel is unique from another standpoint. It practices value investing from a socially responsible set of guidelines. And each of its forty-nine employees owns a piece of the company and is a shareholder in its funds. Founded in 1983 by Rogers, who came to the business with a Princeton education and the encouragement of his prominent attorney parents, Ariel is situated in the eighty-story Aon Center in Chicago, which previously was known as the Amoco Building (until Amoco merged with British Petroleum and downsized the Chicago operation), one of the highest structures on the planet. It's a fitting place for one of the largest minority-owned money management firms in the country.

Rogers loves to talk about the companies he's discovered in recent years as if he has made new friends who have opened new vistas to him. He's like an eight-year-old talking about his Poké-mon collection or the new rollerblades he's mastered. The "names"—money managers typically don't call their holdings *companies*—are not familiar ones to most CNBC addicts: Central Newspapers, General Binding, the Rouse Company, to list a few. Like most value managers, Rogers focuses on brand, competitive positioning, management, and discounted price. One of his favorite companies is Herman Miller, the office equipment manu-facturer based in Michigan. His knitted brow turns smooth as he breaks a gentle smile. "Herman Miller has created a unique cul-ture. They make terrific, innovative products for the small market and they are a leader in their field. The industry has consistently had two dominant players [the dominant behemoth Steelcase] and there's been no shifting sands."

Rogers has held Herman Miller despite the slackness in office furniture and the possibility that a downturn will further stifle growth, which he admits is lower than normal. He bought Herman Miller at what value savants call "an attractive valuation," the right price at the right time. He can live with some variation in the business cycle, or what he calls "moderate cyclicality." Rogers looks at the downside just as carefully as he examines the upside; as such, he tends to be much more conservative than the gunslinging Bill Miller, whom he admires.

Rogers enjoys talking about and with other money managers to swap ideas and exchange stock tips. His friends include well-known managers such as Wally Weitz of the Weitz Value Fund and T. Rowe Price's Preston Athey. And there is also "Warren" [Buffett], "a hero who has that much-admired vision, discipline and ability to communicate why his strategy works."

One of Rogers's "four-baggers" was Central Newspapers, which, until it was acquired by the Gannett Company, was a small newspaper chain that owned the *Arizona Republic* and *Indianapolis Star*, two undeniably middle-market cities. For most fund managers, a company of that size is not even considered. It's not followed closely by Wall Street analysts, it's in a dull-as-drywall industry, and it certainly is not a high-growth company. Where other managers would have shunned Central, Rogers eyeballed management, ran the numbers, and held on. There have been times, like with most value managers, when his strategy or picks simply don't get out of the starting gate, but in times of lean profits, a down-market tends to favor the patient brand of investing Rogers brings to his shareholders.

"With the newspaper business, if there's a downturn, advertising will come back," Rogers observed. "A newspaper has strong cash flow and pricing power." When Rogers refers to pricing power, he's noting a tenet of the Graham-Buffett school that says a worthy company should be able to set prices and have some dominant place in its market. In the case of a newspaper in a one-newspaper town (and Central had two of them), the pricing power comes in the form of advertising and classified rates, which are the backbone of cash flow—and profits.

"With Central Newspapers, we did it right. Phoenix and Indianapolis are two great markets and the CEO did a good job for shareholders. The price of the company doubled last year, but in the beginning it was a real sleeper."

Rogers is also passionate about promoting investing in the community, particularly among African Americans, decrying, "We have no Tiger Woods as a role model in this business." He recalls how his father bought stocks for him for every one of his birthdays after he turned twelve and opened savings and checking accounts for him at Independence Bank on Chicago's South Side. Now he is concerned that not enough African Americans, having climbed the social ladder to become civil servants and beyond, are saving and investing on their own or learning about the stock market. "Savings and investment accumulation is a critical issue for the minority community if there are no safe pension plans or Social Security."

Rogers's style is not for those who want to invest in the hot company du jour. He openly admits that his concentrated portfolio doesn't allow him to "swing the bat too often" by buying and selling stocks. It features low turnover and only buys five to eight stocks per year, so investors expecting dramatic gains every year are going to be disappointed. But Rogers builds wealth while also doing the right thing: his portfolio invests responsibly, both socially and financially.

Well-managed companies that respect the environment, their communities, and their workers tend to be more profitable and avoid government intrusion and costly litigation. This is not a hard and fast rule, but a good place to start.

Being a tortoise has its merits. As of September 30, 2001, the Ariel fund outperformed the S&P 500 Index over a one-, three- and five-year period (value funds almost never best this index). The Ariel fund has also beaten the Russell 2000 value index since inception, annually averaging 14.59 percent, compared to 11.07 percent for the index. And in 2000's massive sell-off, when the S&P 500 was down nearly 10 percent, Ariel was up 28.76 percent. A tortoise shell can be a safe haven at times.

SOCIALLY RESPONSIBLE INVESTING DOS AND DON'TS

Companies that are considered socially responsible:

- Have relatively clean environmental records
- Produce beneficial, safe, and environmentally sound products and services
- Use energy and resources efficiently
- Treat their employees and customers fairly
- Promote women and minorities and place them in top management or board-level positions
- Are involved in community development and charitable giving

Companies that are considered irresponsible:

- Are consistent violators of environmental, employment, and worker safety laws
- Produce weapons, nuclear waste, and defense goods
- Treat their employees badly and pay them sweatshop wages
- Employ inhumane animal testing
- Do business with repressive or authoritative regimes overseas
- Produce unsafe or wasteful products

Why Mid-Cap and Small-Cap Funds
Deserve a Place in Your Portfolio

In a time of sustained growth favoring large companies, small- and mid-cap stocks are going to be outperformed by the big boys. There's little question about that. When the tide turns—and you have no way of predicting when or how—small- and mid-cap stocks are the best place to be. Large-company growth goes through cycles like any business. It simply can't be sustained. That's why small- and mid-cap stocks are ideal additions to your portfolio. Since 1926, if you look at any twenty-year overlapping rolling periods (two-decade consecutive stretches), small-company stocks alone were the highest, with superior returns fifty times compared with six times for large-company stocks. Bonds never were the top-returning asset in this Ibbotson snapshot.

That means, through thick and thin, small-company stocks posted a 21 percent average return. In contrast, if you took the safe course and kept your money in T-bills the whole time, you earned a 7.72 percent return. There is also no question that you needed to take on more risk in the short term to boost your return by a factor of three. The volatility is tremendous at times. You could have lost an average 58 percent in 1937 or gained an average 143 percent in 1933 (a bit of a rebound year in dark times). What happened in more recent times? A combination of mid- and small-cap value would have netted you gains in a bear market (see below).

NO GROWLS HERE: VALUE IN A BEAR MARKET

Category	Return*
Mid-cap value	28%
Small-cap value	20%
Large-cap value	9%
Large-cap growth	−33%
Mid-cap growth	−45%
Small-cap growth	−46%

*Returns of indexes for bear market 2/01/00 to 3/01/01. *Source:* Kanon Bloch Carré, www.kanon.com.

Keep in mind, however, that time heals almost all wounds when it comes to risk. Your small-cap, mid-cap, and large-value funds would have done so-so in a growth-oriented market. When the bear comes along, however, value stocks move to the head of the pack, so it pays to hold them no matter what the short-term market climate is like. The longer you hold a group of stocks, the lower the risk and the greater the chance that you'll make money. I am again speaking of holding breadbaskets of stocks through mutual funds or index mutual funds (discussed in chapter 10 at greater length). Buying a small company or two and holding it doesn't qualify for the long-term risk reduction. In fact, your exposure to risk and volatility is multiplied by holding a small portfolio of stocks.

Portfolio diversification works for small- and mid-cap stocks because they just don't have to meet the expectations that the big boys do. Xerox, Apple, and Amazon.com started out as small-cap companies. They were fresh-faced players who walked onto the field with a promising new way of making money. Investors are smitten with the "theme" of the new player. New players change the way Americans do business. When Xerox exploded on the market, publishers were scared to death that it would make books and printing obsolete. The copy machine giant dominated its market at first, then proceeded to fumble away major research innovations like the computer mouse to other, smaller, more nimble players like Apple Computer.

The Polaroid Corporation, the brainchild of the brilliant investor Edwin Land, burst on the investment scene in the 1960s like a meteor. Instant photography was going to put the mighty giant Kodak out of business. It never happened. Even Kodak stumbled along the way and is trying to claw its way back to the top through digital photography, a field in which it has more than one hundred competitors.

Innovation is a product of corporate culture. If a culture doesn't foster it, then a company can't bring those ideas successfully to market. There are thousands of companies that Wall Street is not paying attention to because they don't have a brand name like Coke, Wal-Mart, or Band-Aid. As Americans, we tend to focus on brands because advertising has permeated our consciousness. We hear and see the ads, a glint of recognition is implanted in our brains, and we buy accordingly.

There are many great products and services that you can miss because small- and mid-cap companies go about their business every day in quiet regions and industries, and the chances of encountering one of their products and gaining that glint of recognition are small. That's why it's smart to hire a mutual fund manager or two to find these smaller companies that are doing business in the global economy. The small-cap companies are often overlooked in favor of Wall Street's darlings, but they may be as profitable as the large caps promoted by brokerage houses. It also makes sense to have a mix of growth and value styles in the mid- and small-cap allocations of your portfolio.

The table below shows how different styles do over time. The middle road between value and growth, called "blend," is the path to moderation and better returns.

RETURNS OF DIFFERENT MARKET CAP FUNDS (1989–2001 SECOND QUARTER)

Style	Value	Blend	Growth
Large	14.8%	15.3%	15.0%
Mid-cap	14.6%	15.2%	15.0%
Small-cap	13.8%	12.2%	10.1%

Source: Frank Russell & Co.

Looking at Style: Value Makes a Difference Again

In a market in which profits are lackluster, merely investing in small or mid caps is not a guaranteed way to make money. Wall Street is constantly looking for earnings reports to show growth. If the growth isn't there, analysts don't recommend the stocks. If the stocks aren't being hawked by the major brokers, then the prices of those stocks aren't bid up. That's perhaps an oversimplified view of reality, but one that explains what happens when earnings slow down in a slack market.

By virtue of their position as typically "out of favor," value stocks have a distinct advantage in slower markets. They've already experienced the dark side of the market. They are off to the sidelines. They have little downside, so that when they surprise the investment community with a turnaround or robust earnings, the market tends to overreact and their share prices go up. The managers who have bought these comeback kids at low prices are not only cheerleaders for these companies—they want to make money— they have been waiting on the sidelines with them, trying to see when they're coming off the bench, how bad their injuries are, and what it would take for them to make the big play.

When growth fell out of favor in the 2000 sell-off, value came from behind to show gains in the face of a slackening economy, layoffs, lower profits (for the large companies), and an increasingly dour consumer and business sentiment. In his annual 401(k) derby of leading funds in retirement plans, financial columnist Scott Burns noted that in December 2000 his list of winners was dominated by growth funds. By August 2001, the tide had turned and seven of the ten funds on his list were value funds.

The most potent gains during the 2000 downturn came from funds that had a small-cap or mid-cap value orientation. You didn't make money if you just picked a small-cap growth fund. The value focus insulated those funds from the sell-off because Wall Street shifted to where it could ferret out profits. Since those managers hadn't been buying companies for earnings alone, they came out ahead.

SMALL-, MID-CAP GROWTH VERSUS VALUE: WHAT HAPPENS IN A MARKET SLIDE

What Happened to a Select Group of Funds Since NASDAQ Sell-off Began on March 10, 2000:

Fund	Return
Small-cap growth funds	−31.88%
Small-cap value funds	+36.54%
Mid-cap funds	+34.97%

Results through 6/30/01. *Source: Wall Street Journal.*

While this is not a full explanation of what happens when a whole capitalization class falls out of favor, it's an argument for having at least a portion of your portfolio tilted toward growth and value in all capitalizations. You can best achieve this through index funds (see chapter 10) or funds that represent both styles in the three capitalizations. It's also important to note that small-cap stocks have an ability to rebound from market slides better than large-cap stocks. In the table below, the index representing small caps is the Russell 2000 Index and large caps are represented by the S&P 500.

SMALL CAPS BOUNCE BACK FROM MARKET SELL-OFFS

Month of Decline	%		Subsequent 12 months	
	Russell 2000	S&P 500	Russell 2000	S&P 500
October '79	−11.1%	−6.4%	55.3%	32.1%
March '80	32.1%	−9.7%	72.1%	40.1%
August '90	40.1%	−21.5%	27.1%	14.8%

Source: Vota Lazard Asset Management.

Scott Vota, who did the research for this table, found that the intense attention paid to the large companies over the past ten years has created opportunities for finding values in small and mid caps. This phenomenon can best be called "who's watching the kids?" Since the big global players like Microsoft and Ford have been soaking up the attention of investors, the smaller companies have been going about their business, but not getting the kind of market attention afforded the larger companies. As a result, Vota observes:

> Given their small market float and, therefore, lower number of owners, reduced trading liquidity [number of people trading the stock] and limited degree of Wall Street analytical coverage, small-cap stocks tend to be less efficiently priced in the market than larger companies . . . the surge in large-cap stocks has not only left small companies behind; it has created a mid-cap asset class that is undervalued and relatively inefficient compared to the largest stocks.

Vota refers to "efficiency" in the sense that all investors know all the facts about a company traded on the stock exchange—and that the stock's price reflects that knowledge. When stocks are "inefficiently" priced, the market may not know everything about the company, and its market value may be less than what the company is actually worth. Value investors are betting constantly that a stock is priced inefficiently so that they can pick up a bargain. By combining a value approach with mid and small caps that are strangers to most investors, you can find more bargains that will eventually rise in value.

If you want to split hairs even further, you can pick even smaller companies called "micro caps" and find even more bargains. The definition of micro caps is extremely fuzzy, but they are generally companies with market capitalizations under $500 million. Picking micro caps is even more difficult than picking mid or small caps because there is even less information available on them and they are thinly traded. Nevertheless, a whole subgroup of fund managers specialize in micro caps, which is the kind of investing you probably needn't try on your own. There are rewards from this kind of investing as well. Of the thirty-eight funds Morningstar identifies as micro-cap funds, twenty-eight posted double-digit gains during the first seven months of 2001, a time when large-cap stocks were being pummeled and were off 19 percent.

SMALL AND MID-CAP STOCKS PULL UP IN BEAR MARKET

Company	Total Return 1/1/2000–12/31/2000	Average Annual Total Return 1/1/1991–12/31/2000
Large company stocks[1]	–9.10%	17.46%
Medium-size company stocks[2]	17.50%	19.86%
Small company stocks[3]	11.81%	17.45%

Measured by: [1]**S&P 500 Stock Index**, an unmanaged index of the stocks of 500 major corporations; [2]**S&P MidCap 400 Index**, an unmanaged index of the stocks of the 400 medium-size corporations; [3]**S&P Small Cap 600 Index**, an unmanaged index of the stocks of 600 small corporations. *Source:* Russell Data Services.

What Small- and Mid-Cap Managers Look For
to Avoid the Crowd

You can start with all of the criteria Bill Miller and John Rogers use. Then add the following to the mix:

- **A sound, growing business.** The business must be making money, although these profits are probably not attracting the attention of most investors.
- **Well-managed companies.** When value managers speak of great companies, they are looking for a holistic blend of quality, innovative management, a unique position in their market, and the ability to survive downturns. These companies are flexible and will do what it takes to survive.
- **A great price.** Based on the traditional Graham/Buffett guidelines, a good place to start is a company trading at 40 percent or more below what the manager believes is a "fair market" value. Analysts look at the total value of all of the company's assets and do a little math to come up with that price.
- **Consistent industries.** You will almost never see a value manager invest in a company in a highly cyclical industry that is constantly being ravaged by business cycles. Paper, chemical, oil, and airline companies almost never make the cut for this reason because they are always hostage to commodity and energy prices. Value managers like to see a company in an industry that can grow at least 15 percent a year—no matter what the economy is doing.
- **Staying away from popular sectors.** Value managers are loath to pick the highflyers just because everyone else is. That's why many value funds did well during the technology rout; the funds didn't own any. If they did, they owned the companies that were underpriced, so they had little downside when the selling began. If anything, value managers tend to be contrarians; they place their bet on the horse that few others will bet on.
- **Middle and small companies that are merger or buyout candidates.** Value managers know that if they do their job, their purchase will signal to other companies that their holdings are

worthwhile investments. So it's not unusual for their prize holdings to be snapped up by bigger fish.

TOP MID- AND SMALL-CAP FUNDS

Fund	5-year Return	Phone
Mid-caps		
Oakmark Select I	26.45%	(800) 625-6275
Vanguard Capital Opportunity	20.38%	(800) 662-7447
Weitz Value	20.99%	(800) 232-4161
Small caps		
T. Rowe Price Small Cap	11.98%	(800) 638-5660
Royce Premier	12.48%	(800) 221-4268
Vanguard Small-Cap* Value Index	12.43%	(800) 662-7447

Period (annualized) ending 12/31/01. *3-year annualized return. *Source:* Morningstar.

John Rogers's playful allusion to the tortoise and the hare is well suited to his philosophy and describes two of the traits for a successful investor—patience and knowledge of human nature. That reminds me of another Aesop fable, which more pointedly reflects upon what happens when people make bad decisions.

A threadbare spendthrift who had spent his fortune saw a swallow in early spring. Believing that summer had come and that he could do without his coat, he sold his coat. Summer, however, was not there yet, and a sharp frost came along and killed the swallow. When the spendthrift saw the dead bird, he cried, "Thanks to you, I am perishing of cold myself." Although Aesop, a Greek slave who lived around 600 B.C., commented, "One swallow does not a summer make," an updated view would be, "Take your time, prepare for cold weather, and stop buying on stock tips you hear on television or from your brother-in-law."

CHAPTER 7

Values Abroad: And You Thought the Best Investments Were in the United States?

The old thought that one cannot be rich except at the expense of his neighbor, must pass away. True prosperity adds to the richness of the whole world, such as that of the man who makes two trees grow where only one grew before. The parasitical belief in prosperity as coming by the sacrifices of others has no place in the mind that thinks true. "My benefit is your benefit, your success is my success," should be the basis of all our wealth.

Anne Rix Militz

Leah Joy Zell is the kind of person who would succeed running a megacorporation, chairing a history department at an Ivy League college, or holding a Cabinet post. Her intelligence and confident élan radiate from her like a high-tension electrical line. In her role as manager of the Liberty Acorn International Fund, she has the job of finding ways to invest more than $2 billion across the world in small- and mid-cap companies. Like John Rogers and Bill Miller, she is largely a value player, but she focuses on overseas companies that have market capitalizations under $5 billion. She spends most of her time traveling between the countries where she has the top-five allocations: the United Kingdom, Switzerland, Japan, Germany, and Canada. She has more frequent-flyer miles than time to spend them.

Taut with short hair and wire-rimmed glasses, Leah Zell takes her time to compose her sentences as if every one of them is to be written out in elegant prose. With continents to consider, she does the mental calculus of finding bargains across different economies, reading prospectuses in different languages, diversifying across several industries, and dealing with the fluctuations of several currencies. Holding a Ph.D. from Harvard in modern European social and economic history, she's an unabashed expert on how Europe and Japan rebuilt after World War II. With that unique perspective, she knows the landscape with an academic, disciplined sense of history. Although she is brimming with investment ideas, Zell doesn't have to go far to discuss investing. Her husband and partner, Ralph Wanger, is the revered manager of the Liberty Acorn Fund, a small-cap domestic fund. Her brother, Sam Zell, is the legendary real estate mogul also known as "the grave dancer" for his prowess in finding properties at fire-sale prices.

Balance is a powerful theme in Zell's work. Her Harvard dissertation concentrated on finding a workable balance of economic growth and stability in the postwar era. As a value investor, she is constantly seeking the ideal medium between price and the intrinsic value of a company. Due to the objective of her fund, she has to look for that delicate combination outside the sphere of powerful international companies like Nestlé, Philips, Daimler, and Nokia. Instead, she focuses her research on lesser-known companies like the Serco Group, Li & Fung, Autogrill, and Capita Group. Her fund contains no more than 20 percent of its holdings in any one industry; it's diversified across business services, consumer goods/services, financial services, broadcasting/media, and industrials.

"I look for stable yet dynamic companies. I have an intuitive sense of what's stable. If a company isn't satisfying a real demand at a reasonable price, imbalances will always right themselves," she notes, referring to the market's propensity to reward investors who are buying financially sound companies at a good price.

Zell is thriving relative to her competition and foreign stock funds in general. It hasn't been easy for any international fund in recent years, either. Economic turmoil has continued not only in Japan for the eleventh straight year, Southeast Asia has been hit hard, along with South America (particularly Argentina) and Russia. Although she sticks with the countries with the most durable economies, returns for international funds have been paltry relative to the booming returns seen on Wall Street. The index to which she compares her fund's performance—the SSB EMI (Global ex-US) Index—has shown a negative 0.39 percent return over the past five years and a loss of more than 2 percent over the last three years. A piggy bank shows a better return. Zell's fund, however, has returned 9.98 percent over the past five years and 13.44 percent over the last decade, trouncing the index average. Those returns are remarkable given the fact that 8.5 percent of her fund is in Japan and Europe, which didn't post the same stellar returns as the United States during the 1990s. She attributes her performance to the same reason the tortoise beat the hare.

"We build our investing strategy around patience," she says with her wry smile. "The media wants us to be in the right asset class all of the time, but my job is to invest in small-cap equities all of the time."

Zell likens her research mission to "history turned inside out." History has ready information that needs to be interpreted. Analyzing a stock requires starting with a story or a hypothesis on where the company is going and filling in the gaps. Managers call the story "themes," which are leitmotifs in a company's ascent to market recognition. For example, she has explored the theme of corporate outsourcing, a situation in which a company decides not to pursue a line of business on its own and contracts it out to another company, usually because the service or product can be provided at a lower cost. Zell then bought a few companies that performed contract manufacturing as a play upon that theme. These companies had decent profits and ran at 100 percent capacity, so the economics were compelling. Then she sold those holdings as they became overpriced (in terms of p/e ratios).

"Does the theme have 'legs'? Is the concept valid? That's what we ask ourselves." Zell also walks her analysts through the standard retinue of the value gauntlet: "What is the quality of the management? How is the business franchise? Does the company have a good balance sheet? I don't like balance sheet risk [high debt levels relative to equity, the debt to equity ratio]."

Zell reduces portfolio risk by having not more than 8 percent of her portfolio in any one stock and diversifying across countries, regions, and industries. After the fund lost a fifth of its value in 2000, she sold off half of her technology holdings and boosted exposure to more stable sectors such as health care, financials, and energy. Although short-term, the firm takes an average amount of risk; it's had slack years in the mid-'90s and a Katie-bar-the-door year in 1999, when it rocketed 79 percent. Because of its high volatility—its standard deviation is 27 percent—you can't jump in and out of this fund. It's like going to London or Paris for an afternoon. You spend more time on the plane and getting fogged by jet lag than you do on the Champs-Elysée. Nevertheless, despite the volatility, a steady holding in this fund over a three- to five-year period will probably see you outperform 75 percent of her competition.

With her characteristic confidence, she comes off a losing year with an eye on history, which tends to be in her favor. "International small caps outperform large caps over time. It's a shame to sell small companies in the middle of their growth trajectory. It's time to recycle dollars into less well-known companies. I believe in riding winners."

Small and Mid Caps across the Ocean: Growth on the Other Side of the Big Pond

Most investors are so fixated on Wall Street, they have no idea what lies beyond the Big Board at Broad and Wall. The United States is no longer the juggernaut in manufacturing and services it was; the rest of the world has caught up. Manufacturing has left

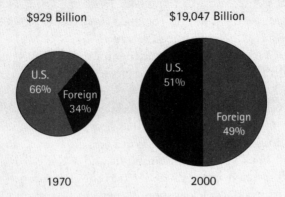

WORLD STOCK MARKET CAPITALIZATION

For the 22 countries represented in the MSCI World Index

$929 Billion $19,047 Billion

1970   2000

Source: Morgan Stanley Capital International (MSCI).

our shores for places like the People's Republic of China and Brazil. Heavy manufacturing (vehicles, machine tools, steel, etc.) has taken the biggest one-way ticket to foreign shores. The shift has been so dramatic that the U.S. share of the world's gross domestic product—the total output of all goods and services— dropped to 40 percent in 2000, down from more than 50 percent in 1970. As a result, foreign stock markets now represent 49 percent of the world's $19 trillion in stock capitalization, up from a 34 percent share in 1970.

Even more surprising is the diversification of the economies outside of the United States. Although most services are still based here, manufacturing has seen a startling shift to overseas factories. Here's a sampling:

MAJOR INDUSTRIES NOW OVERSEAS

- 9 of the 10 largest appliance manufacturers (only Whirlpool is based in the United States)
- 8 of the 10 largest metals companies (more steel is made abroad now)
- 7 of the 10 largest vehicle manufacturers (good-bye "Big Three")
- 7 of the 10 largest electronics companies (no more VCRs or TVs made in the United States)
- 5 of the 10 largest telecommunications companies (look at your cell phone)

Source: MSCI, RIMES Technologies, T. Rowe Price, January 30, 2001.

Following the cyclical nature of markets, foreign stock markets have their day in the sun, but not in recent years. Foreign markets have handily outperformed the U.S. market in years in which domestic growth wasn't as strong as it was in the late 1990s. In fact, the curve that shows foreign markets outperforming U.S. markets during sluggish times at home is one of the most compelling reasons to add foreign stocks to your portfolio. The zigzag curve of foreign-to-U.S. performance is a billboard for diversification and lowering portfolio risk.

From 1981 through 1994, for example, foreign stocks as measured by the Morgan Stanley EAFE (Europe, Australia, Far East) Index soundly outperformed the U.S. market, as measured by the S&P 500 in ten-year rolling periods. The Morgan Stanley index lumps in economies as dour as Japan with solid performers like Switzerland, so what you're getting is a broad average.

You need to look at when those foreign markets were doing well to get an idea why it's good to be in foreign stocks. The EAFE index outperformed U.S stocks in the early and mid-'70s when stocks were dismal investments in the United States, during periods of the mid-'80s (and after the 1987 crash), and in a brief spurt in 1992–1993. In terms of correlation—the statistic that tells you how often two numbers move in the same direction—only Canada had a high degree of correlation between 1970 and 2000 (72 percent). The Pacific region moves with the U.S. market about 37 percent of the time, Europe about 58 percent of the time. Overall, the EAFE breadbasket of foreign stocks travels down the same road as the United States slightly more than half of the time.

In the sensible scheme of diversification, it's ideal to be seeing some returns overseas when things are not so good here. Globalization has caused more of our markets to follow the path of overseas markets, but some inverse correlation (moves in the opposite direction) is always a solid way to reduce the overall risk of your portfolio.

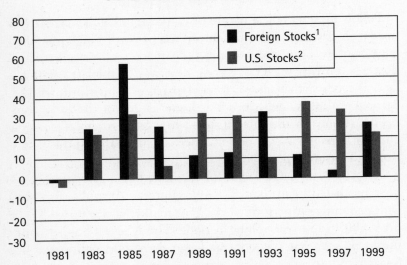

U.S. STOCKS VERSUS FOREIGN STOCKS

Foreign Stocks[1]
U.S. Stocks[2]

1. Morgan Stanley Capital International EAFE Index (Europe, Australia, and Far East Developed Market Index)

2. S&P 500 Index

Source: T. Rowe Price, January 30, 2001.

Risks of Overseas Investing

The diversification from foreign stocks comes with a little price tag. You'll encounter two unique forms of risk that you don't have investing in U.S. stocks: *currency* risk and *political* risk. Foreign stocks are denominated in the currencies of the countries of origin. Most European stocks, however, are denominated in the euro, a pan-European currency that follows the dollar fairly closely. Like all currencies, the euro is subject to daily changes in value. More than $1 trillion goes through currency markets every business day. Banks buy and sell currencies and futures contracts designed to lock in values on those currencies. Investors speculate or hedge on currencies depending on whether they think—or hope—they'll go up or down in a short period of time.

For example, if you're a big institutional money manager, you can buy shares in Daimler, the huge German vehicle company that owns Chrysler and Mercedes-Benz. You buy those shares in euros and you don't want the euros to fall in value relative to the U.S. dollar. So you either take the chance that the currency doesn't get hurt, or you "hedge" by buying futures contracts that lock in a certain price level of the euro, which ensures that you don't lose money on the currency if it falls. The currency fluctuation adds a complex level of risk to foreign investments because the currency markets are as unpredictable as the stock market and are pegged to interest rates throughout the world. So you could make money in a foreign stock, but lose money on the currency "translation" into U.S. dollars. Since there's no way to avoid this risk, you have to pick a fund manager who's not too concentrated in one country or region.

That brings us to the subject of political risk. The stability of a country's economy largely depends on the people running the government and finance sector, namely the central banks. All of the largest industrial economies have fairly strong central governments and banks. Once you get beyond Japan, Germany, Canada, Great Britain, France, Holland, Italy, the Scandinavian countries, and Spain, you enter a world in which huge currency devaluations and inflation are a constant source of economic torment. South American economies are consistently battling inflation, which ravages the industries that do business there. Indonesia and countries doing business with it are still hurting from a free fall in their currency a few years ago. And then there's Japan.

Japan is trying to work itself through a bubble that burst eleven years ago when it had billions pouring out of overvalued stock and real estate markets. It may be years still before the country rebounds. Smart investors like Leah Zell, however, know that there are some tremendous values in Japan and other ravaged economies, so that's another reason to favor a patient overseas diversification scheme that includes the Pacific, Europe, and South America. Sooner or later Japan will turn around and the People's Republic of China will be a prudent place to invest. You need a qualified mutual fund manager to get you there.

There are also choices within international funds from which to choose style and capitalization. Zell, for example, is a specialist in small- to mid-cap value stocks overseas. As with domestic stocks, there's a sizable advantage in choosing value over growth, as the table below indicates:

VALUE OVERSEAS: A WINNER

Category	Annual Return (1973–2000)
Foreign large value	15.5%
Foreign small cap	13.9%
Foreign large cap growth	11.7%

Source: www.tamasset.com.

Types of International Stock Funds

Like U.S. funds, foreign funds can get highly specialized. I suggest that you seek as much diversification as possible to avoid region or country risk. The following table outlines the kinds of funds and the relative risks they incur.

FUNDS AND THEIR RELATIVE RISKS

Type of Fund	Strategy	Risk Level
International growth and income	Combines stocks and income	Low to moderate
International stock fund	Long-term growth of non-U.S. firms	Moderate
Global stock fund	Growth companies may include United States	Moderate
Small-company value	Value-oriented foreign companies	Low to moderate
International bond	Overseas bonds	Moderate
European stock	European growth companies	Moderate
Emerging markets	Companies in emerging economies	High
Regional funds	Stocks in regions like Latin America, Asia	Highest
Single-country funds	Stocks in specific countries like Japan	Highest

How Much Should You Own in Foreign Funds?

Just as you would not build a portfolio made of only one stock, bond, or piece of real estate, you would not want your portfolio dominated by foreign stocks. Every portfolio needs to have some foreign stocks. How much depends upon how much risk and volatility you can tolerate.

As a rule, the more conservative portfolios have no more than 15 percent of the total allocation in foreign stocks. The most aggressive portfolios have no more than 40 percent in overseas issues. Since you need room for large-cap, mid-cap, and small-company stocks, bonds, real estate, and cash, it would be imprudent to suggest that foreign stocks would *ever* account for more than 45 percent of your holdings.

Those who think they can "time" a bull market for foreign stocks are constantly looking at last year's hot performers and missing the boat. I can tell you from personal experience how things can turn out badly. In the mid-1990s, the investment world was tittering at the prospect of "emerging markets" as the next big engine of growth. Countries like Singapore, Indonesia, and Malaysia were referred to as "Asian Tigers," even though they had tiny stock markets and were subject to huge swings in local currencies.

Nevertheless, trillions poured into these countries and mutual funds sprouted up like mushrooms after a June rain to trumpet the gains from emerging economies. That's when investors like me thought they were going to make a quick 60 percent to 100 percent return through emerging markets mutual funds. As is the case most of the time, the mutual funds and brokers did much better than I did. I bought into several funds advertising stellar returns from the *prior* year. After a so-so year, most of those "tigers" had turned into scared mice and their currencies were plundered by investors moving their money to other places and speculators who added to the economic carnage. Because the Asian money was moving so fast and furious back to safer Western shores, Alan Greenspan fiddled with the money supply and interest rates to avert a market meltdown, but those markets have yet to recover. After a few losing and subpar years, I exited my international funds, tail between my legs, so to speak.

Having shared with you one of the cardinal rules of investing— *don't* invest based on last year's performance—I can still heartily endorse some stake in overseas markets. The fact that they are not always moving in the same direction as U.S. stocks is one of the best reasons to think that if there's a bear market in the United States, holding foreign stocks will give you positive returns.

Professor Meir Statman, who teaches finance at Santa Clara University, has calculated how portfolios composed of various proportions of foreign stocks and U.S. large caps, small caps, bonds, and cash performed from 1969 through 1997. Here's what he found:

A DIVERSIFIED PORTFOLIO EMPLOYING FOREIGN STOCKS*

Type of Investment	Conservative	Moderate	Aggressive
Large-company stocks	17.0%	39.0%	57.0%
Small stocks	0	0	2.0%
Foreign stocks	13.0%	23.0%	41.0%
Bonds	31.0%	38.0%	0
Cash	39.0%	0	0
Annual Return	**9.5%**	**11.8%**	**13.7%**
Volatility	**5.8%**	**11.0%**	**16.2%**

*Based on historical returns of various indices 1969–1997. *Source:* Meir Statman, *AAII Journal.*

With this example, you see that the more risk you take, the greater the return, and vice versa. I would beg to differ with the professor on the allocations. I think that every investor—no matter how conservative—needs to have some small-company stocks because of the outstanding long-term returns. The larger point is that adding foreign stocks will boost returns. For most investors, the proper amount falls between 10 percent and 25 percent.

What you need to achieve with international funds is an *efficient frontier*, a state in which you are reaping the maximum amount of return for the lowest amount of risk. Generally, investing your portfolio in no more than 30 percent foreign stocks will give you the benefits of diversification while boosting returns. This percentage varies over time, so it's a starting place.

BEST INTERNATIONAL FUNDS

Fund	5-year Return	Phone
Artisan International	12.32%	(800) 344-1770
Liberty-Acorn International Z	5.57%	(800) 322-2847
T. Rowe Price International Discovery	9.76%	(800) 638-5660

Period (annualized) ending 12/31/01. *Source:* Morningstar.

What Do You Do When an Asset Class Hits a Bad Year?

Like U.S. stocks, foreign stocks will hit their bad patches. Since they run in cycles of several consecutive years (this is typical but not always true), you can count on some underperformance when U.S. stocks are roaring. My suggestion is that you keep the foreign stock allocation at your comfort level. A 10 percent allocation is best for those who don't want to feel much pain; up to 30 percent is fine if you feel especially adventurous. If you see a fund hit double-digit losses—and that doesn't feel right—then switch to more conservatively managed funds, but keep in mind the manager's long-term record. Zell's fund, for example, had an awful year in 2000, but that doesn't mean you should abandon her fund, because her investment style often takes years to reap rewards. It all depends on how patient you are.

You can no more predict which country or region will have a good run than you can foresee which U.S. market sector will do well. International investing becomes even more prickly when you take into account political, currency, and regional risks. Understanding international investing is, in the words of Charles Morris, "the murky depths of the economy. Like a plumbing system, it is invisible when it is working well, but a broken pipe can be a disaster."

As with so many other types of investments, it's impossible to predict where countries and regions are going to be from year to year, so you need to hold them for at least five to ten years to take advantage of cycles that will eventually run in your favor. It will be a pleasant surprise when the other shoe drops in the U.S. market.

■   ■   ■

Speaking of shoes, have you heard the Brothers Grimm's tale about the elves and the shoemaker? There once was a poor shoemaker who had leather enough for only one pair of shoes. Exhausted from thinking about his ill fortune, he went to sleep that night, leaving the pair of shoes unfinished. Rising that next day, having faith that things would turn around (he had also said his prayers the night before), he found a perfectly sewn pair of new shoes sitting on his cobbler's bench. They were masterfully crafted, with not a stitch out of place. A buyer soon appeared for the shoes and paid twice the normal price for them because of the outstanding craftsmanship. Now the cobbler could afford enough leather for two pairs of shoes, which he cut out before he went to bed. The next morning, the shoes were finished again and were as exquisite as the original pair.

Naturally, the cobbler and his wife were more than curious as to how the shoes were being made in the dead of night by unseen hands, so they hid in a corner and waited the next night. At midnight, they saw two naked elves come into the workshop and finish the shoes. They didn't stop until they had finished their work, then ran swiftly away. The couple went to bed and had a discussion of the night's events the next morning. "Since the elves brought us prosperity, we should make them fine shoes and clothing." And so they did and laid out the garments and shoes and waited until midnight. The elves saw the charming clothes and footwear, put them on, and did a joyous dance in utter delight. They leapt around the room in glee, then scurried out the door, to be seen no more. The cobbler and wife, however, still fared well in all that they did.

There are happy, industrious elves lurking in the market. They are foreign to us, but they are there, nevertheless. We never see them, nor can we predict when—or where—they'll bring us prosperity. You just have to wait for them to show up and do their handiwork.

CHAPTER 8

Doing It Yourself: An Integrated Approach to Stocks

Oh money, money, money
I'm not necessarily one of those who thinks thee holy,
But I often stop to wonder
How thou canst go out so fast when thou comest in so slowly.
— Ogden Nash

Having spent a great deal of this book extolling mutual funds and the value school of investing, I'd like to take you down a different road. *You* can build a portfolio of growth stocks on your own— and make money with moderate risk. To those who grew up thinking only a broker, banker, or money manager should be touching money, this may be quite a turnabout.

I've spent untold hours meeting with individual investors who've been successful at building their own portfolios. They don't use complicated formulas to pick their own stocks and they certainly have no expectation of beating the market. These "self-reliant" investors build portfolios of largely dividend-producing stocks that grow over time.

In this regard, I've also had some experience. My wife and I have been picking individual stocks—in addition to our mutual funds—for the past six years as part of our family investment club,

"The Wall Street Prowlers." It's been an educating and often-trying experience, as we've lost family members to disinterest, divorce, and other concerns. After a watershed year in 1999, the years 2000 and 2001 proved especially challenging as we watched nearly all of our holdings get clobbered. Undaunted, we not only stayed the course and held on to every one of our stocks (GE, Walgreens, RPM, Sysco, Oracle, ADC Telecom, Merck, and Motorola), and we bought more stocks in some of the most bruised and battered issues. ADC Telecom, which dropped from $40 a share to $3 a share, hurt the most, but our faith in the company's prospects made us buyers, not sellers. Although the value of our portfolio dropped by nearly 25 percent in a year's time, we are long-term buy-and-hold investors. We chose our stocks after months of research; unless the companies do something drastically wrong, we're going to hold until somebody in the club needs to cash out.

George Fisher is perhaps the best example of someone who has done it on his own, with no connection to the world of high finance, mutual funds, or money management. Fisher has hustled most of his life. For fourteen years he sold roofing and molding materials for Georgia-Pacific. He quit that job in his mid-thirties to buy a company that made water pumps. The company made money, but the ninety-five-year-old founder and sixty-five-year-old son running it had seen better days. Fisher and his father-in-law turned it around, getting sales to grow 25 percent a year, before selling it in 1989.

Starting his own company, Fisher then decided to become a manufacturer's representative for Tecumseh engines, specializing in pump engines for the Asian market. He helped farmers keep water flowing in rice paddies throughout the Philippines, Indonesia, Singapore, Malaysia, Thailand, Cambodia, Vietnam, Taiwan, and Korea. He would travel to Asia two or three times a year and visit seven or eight cities each time he went. Although not every pump could be adapted to the Asian market, Fisher did well until 1997, when a combination of factory overcapacity and the Asian currency collapse took its toll. After the meltdown, the engines he sold cost twice as much in local currencies as they had before the debacle.

He was also up against tenacious Japanese competition, which was quick to offer creative financing. His business evaporated.

After "getting sick of writing please hire me letters" in 1997, Fisher decided to start a new business. He had been investing on his own since 1970 and was determined to turn that into a new enterprise. A newsletter focusing on stocks that offered dividend-reinvestment plans (DRIPs)—*Power Investing with DRIPs*—became his new undertaking. He would offer one of three newsletters with advice on DRIPs, and was certainly the unproven new kid on the block. Having been chastened by "thousands of dollars of losses using brokers' advice in the 1970s," Fisher was determined to find a low-cost strategy that worked.

DRIPs are offered by companies as a way of keeping investors engaged in the company's progress. Generally, DRIPs are available from established companies that pay out a percentage of profits in the form of a dividend; DRIPs allow investors the chance to reinvest that dividend in new shares. The little bonus that DRIPs offer is that all new shares bought with reinvested quarterly dividends—or by writing a check—are purchased *at no commission.* This is the company's way of saying "Thanks for investing, and by the way, would you like another helping of our shares?"

Fisher likes DRIPs because there are a wide variety of them in nearly every industry. DRIPs were originally born in the 1960s to help companies build capital by cultivating a loyal base of investors. Some seventeen hundred public companies offer DRIPs, all of which only require that you buy one share to get into the plan. Since the Securities and Exchange Commission relaxed the rules regarding DRIPs in the mid-'90s, these plans have exploded in number and popularity. The plans are simple in design: You buy the shares, which are held by a "transfer agent," usually a bank. The transfer agent handles all of the transactions and recordkeeping and you get a statement every quarter.

Better yet, a growing group of companies also offer direct investment plans, or "DIPs," which will sell you that first share directly, so you pay no commission for any shares you purchase from those companies. Some notable DIPs are offered by McDonald's and Chevron Texaco. It may seem dangerous to buy stock directly from the issuer—after all, aren't we trained to call our brokers, bankers, or money managers for advice on the most insignificant financial detail?

Fisher estimates that of the 45 million Americans who invest in the stock market, only 5 million know about DRIPs and DIPs. Not only do DRIPs and DIPs give you a virtually low-cost way to invest, they give you access to thousands of quality, brand-name companies like General Electric, Merck, and Wal-Mart. In fact, DIPs in particular offer individual investors advantages not even mutual funds can boast—they can buy stocks at no commission for very low initial investments. Because DRIPs allow you to invest at such a low cost, Fisher says he "hates mutual funds as an investment vehicle." He offers this example of how mutual fund fees can eat up returns over a lifetime:

> Let's say Joe Investor invested $10,000 every 10 years in stock mutual funds from age thirty until age sixty. He has paid 1.5 percent every year to the funds to manage his money. He retires at age sixty and discontinues his fund contributions, letting the money accumulate until age eighty-five, when he passes away with a smile on his face. He's made 11 percent on his funds—in line with the historic return for the S&P Index. He's left his heirs $2,437,797, not bad for an investment of $40,000. Had Joe invested in DRIPs at an 11 percent annual return, however, he would have turned in his grave. His DRIP portfolio would be worth $5,246,893. Over his lifetime, he's paid a total of $430,000 in fund fees.

Since you start out with one share and there's no requirement to buy additional shares, you can build a DRIP portfolio with very little money. Most mutual funds require that you open a fund with at least $2,000; some of the larger funds now require $25,000 or more. If you don't have that much money to commit, then DRIPs are often a sensible way to start off a long-term investing plan.

WHAT DRIPS AND DIPS COST

Although there are typically no commissions associated with DRIPs and DIPs, nearly every plan charges a transaction fee per purchase or sale. A handful of plans even charge a small commission. Fisher says 60% of the companies he follows only charge fees when shares are sold. Here's a range of small fees charged by DRIPs and DIPs:

FEE RANGE FOR DIPS AND DRIPS

Type of Fee	Amount
Setup fees	$5 to $15 to establish account
Termination fees	$5 to $15 when you sell all shares
Commissions	From $0.15 to $2 per share

Source: Power Investing with DRIPs.

DRIPs are also extremely popular among investment clubs, small groups of investors who pool their money to buy stocks for the long term. (If you want to know more about investment clubs, consult my *Kitchen-Table Investor* or *Investment Club Book*.) Whether you are with a club or on your own, the DRIP is the natural vehicle to anchor your portfolio because you can invest as little or as much as you want every quarter through "optional cash investments."

Using his own numerical rating system, Fisher selects DRIPs for a variety of portfolios that are screened for risk. His conservative portfolio usually consists of old-line companies that are paying consistent dividends. More aggressive portfolios focus on companies whose financial ratings may not be as strong as the older companies, but are poised for growth. This is an outline of his rating system:

- Start out with the best managed companies. They should have at least ten years of earnings growth and dividend payments.

- Look for the Standard & Poor's (S&P) equity ranking. The S&P system rates companies using a letter scale, "A+" being the highest and "not rated" being questionable. Fisher prefers "A+" to "B+" companies. The S&P reports are available in the business reference sections of most libraries. Fisher notes that by only selecting "A+" companies, you eliminate 90 percent of the companies offering DRIPs.

- Look for companies that are priced favorably for today's market. Has the company recently dropped in S&P ranking? Have the earnings estimates and returns on equity been below industry averages? These companies may be bargains.

- Fisher likes companies that are growing 20 percent a year, although those companies may be hard to find in a slack economy. Ideally, these companies are paying out no more than 65 percent of their earnings in dividends. This "dividend payout ratio" is a calculation he uses to find companies that are paying dividends, yet retaining enough earnings to grow their business.

- Are earnings consistently growing over the past decade? Spotty earnings records are good ways to weed out inconsistent management. "Excellent management will always find a way to make a profit. These are the companies you need to be investing in."

- What are the consensus brokers' estimates for earnings? Look at earnings estimates for this year and next year. Is the company still growing? Check out www.zacks.com (an independent research firm) or www.morningstar.com for analysts' opinions.

- The company's current p/e ratio should be below the average of its five-year range and below industry averages. This is one way of spotting a company that is underpriced.

- Look at the company's next year PEG ratio, also known as the Y-PEG. This number shows the relationship between the current p/e ratio to the company's anticipated earnings-per-share (EPS) growth rate. The PEG formula is the current price divided by the current EPS divided by the anticipated EPA growth rate. Although this sounds complicated, PEG ratios provide a glimpse into how a company may grow its earnings. When the p/e ratio equals EPS estimates, the PEG is 1.00. Any PEG under 1.00 is considered a

HOW MUCH TO INVEST MONTHLY TO
RETIRE A MILLIONAIRE

Starting	Interest rate of annual return		
at age	8%	10%	12%
25	$287	$159	$85
30	$436	$264	$156
35	$671	$443	$287
40	$1,052	$754	$533
45	$1,698	$1,317	$1,011
50	$2,890	$2,413	$2,002
55	$5,467	$4,882	$4,348
60	$13,610	$12,914	$12,245

It's no secret that the earlier you start investing for retirement, the better off you'll be because of a little thing called compound interest. But just to illustrate how important it is to start planning your retirement now, rather than later, I have calculated how much you'd need to invest monthly, at different rates (historically, the stock market average has been about 10% annually), in order to reach a million by the traditional retirement age of 65.

Source: Your Money.

good value and should be considered for a purchase if all of the other factors line up. A PEG of 0.5 or less is considered a great value. You can find PEG ratios at www.aaii.org or in investment reference materials in the library.

"Investing is about finding value in top-quality companies," Fisher explains, sounding like investing icon Benjamin Graham. Offering model portfolios of his favorite DRIPs, Fisher claims that his best portfolio returned 18 percent in 2000 when the overall market lost money. Since he doesn't manage other people's money, his numbers are not audited, but his overall approach features lower risk than most stock mutual funds. Nevertheless, you don't need to read his newsletter to find great DRIPs to invest in for your portfolio, although his approach is a worthwhile launching pad. It's a truly integrated method for the self-reliant investor. If this is the kind of research you will relish, then sample his cooking.

Why DRIPs Make Sense If You Want to Do the Homework

You can literally build your own mutual fund with DRIPs. Like a truly diversified mutual fund, however, it makes sense to build your portfolio so that it includes stocks from a number of different industries. It would be unwise—and highly risky—to concentrate all of your DRIPs in utilities, food service, or financial services in case the market turns against those sectors. Start off with companies you understand. Utilities are a natural first step. You know what they do and how they do it. They typically pay higher-than-average dividends and nearly every established utility has a DRIP. Some groups are so broad that they include subsectors. Financial services is a case in point. Within that group you have companies ranging from those that are cash machines, like insurers, to those that are highly sensitive to the economy, like retail stock brokers.

Here are some often recession-resilient industries that you can consider when diversifying your DRIP portfolio. If you had one stock from each of the following industry groups, you'd be fairly well diversified.

- **Utilities.** Electrical, telephone/telecom, gas, and water all pay healthy dividends.
- **Financial services.** Some of the oldest institutions have the steadiest dividend payments. These include all types of insurers (property, life, brokers), retail banks, savings and loans, stock brokers, investment banks, and "nonbank" finance companies. The older, more established banks and insurers hold up particularly well during a recession.

- **Manufacturers.** There are thousands of manufacturers that have been around for fifty years or more. Some are well known, like GE; others make more obscure products, like Illinois Tool Works.
- **Food and food service.** Always reliable stocks in a downturn because they hold their value and pay a steady dividend, and people still buy food when times are bad.
- **Energy.** Natural gas and oil producers, oil service, and energy traders typically channel their profits into reliable dividends.
- **Retail.** These are among the most visible companies because they are in nearly every commercial district. They include Wal-Mart, The Home Depot, and Walgreens.
- **Technology/telecom.** This is perhaps the most sensible way of investing in tech stocks. You can buy low and hold on.
- **Materials and industrial companies.** No big names here, but they make everything from paint to oil rigs.
- **Tobacco.** If you don't mind owning these stocks, they are among the most consistent dividend payers around.
- **Defense manufacturers.** Again, if this passes your ethical screen, you can count on dividends because these companies usually have a steady book of orders from Uncle Sam.

Employing Dollar-Cost Averaging: You Don't Have to Time the Market

When's the best time to buy a DRIP? After you've done your research and selected a quality company. Remember, you want to hold this company for several years, so the idea is to buy a business that you won't want to sell until you really need the money. A DRIP portfolio is the opposite of cash. It's not for money you'll need within the next ten years or more if you do things right. (A personal note: My wife and I have a family investment club that employs DRIPs. We hope to use the proceeds for our two daughters' college educations, which are about fifteen years down the road at this writing.)

A SAMPLING OF STEADY DIVIDEND PAYERS:
STOCKS THAT HAVE CONSISTENTLY PAID DIVIDENDS
FOR AT LEAST 15 YEARS

Stock	Dividend Paid Since	Dividend Yield
Abbott Labs	1926	1.6%
Anheuser Busch	1932	1.6%
BB&T Corporation	1934	2.6%
Exxon Mobil	1882	2.0%
FleetBoston Financial	1791	3.7%
Hormel Foods	1928	2.2%
Jefferson Pilot	1913	2.1%
PPG Industries	1899	2.6%
Philip Morris	1928	4.8%
Progress Energy	1937	4.4%

Source: Standard & Poor's.

The best tool to employ when buying DRIPs is dollar-cost averaging (see table on page 126). This is a fairly simple technique that allows you to buy stocks on a regular basis, without timing the market or worrying about whether you are buying in at a peak or valley. You just keep buying.

What this dollar-cost-averaging example shows is that you avoid buying all your shares at the market's peak in November and buy more shares when the stock price sells off. Since you can never guess correctly when a stock price will hit its high or low for the year, this way of investing gets you more shares when the price is down.

But What about Taxes? Aren't Capital Gains Better than Dividends?

The tax laws change every few years to reflect shifts in politics and investing strategies. The last wave of tax-code changes reduced estate taxes and capital gains taxes. While the estate taxes are only reduced until 2010 (try to die before then if you want to leave a

DOLLAR-COST AVERAGING: BUY LOW AND HIGH AND HOLD

$50 a Month in American Pie, Inc.

Month	Stock Price
January	$9.00
February	$11.50
March	$12.00
April	$10.00
May	$8.00
June	$9.50
July	$8.50
August	$9.00
September	$10.50
October	$11.00
November	$12.00
December	$8.00

Average Purchase Price: $9.92
Amount Invested: $600

---

bigger pile for your heirs), the capital gains taxes will be as low as 10 percent, depending on your tax bracket. Your marginal tax rate roughly reflects what you're going to pay, up to a maximum of 20 percent.

Capital gains are increases in the value of what you own through appreciation, typically through a rise in market value. Dividends, however, didn't get the same favors from Congress and are taxed as ordinary income, the same as your wages at your marginal rate. So if you are taxed at the 33 percent level (28 percent federal and 5 percent state taxes), that's what the government will take if you are paid dividends. It hardly seems fair.

At one time in the not-so-distant past, the first $700 of dividends were exempt from income taxes and capital gains were taxed at higher rates. That was during a time when dividend-paying stocks were held by people who never sold them and relied on them for retirement income. You probably know someone in your family who owned AT&T for the dividend and died, leaving someone to inherit it. Now there's double taxation on dividends: both the corporation and you have to pay taxes on them.

Because of the current tax code favoring capital gains taxation over dividends, income-paying stocks lost a lot of sizzle and newer, higher-flying companies invested profits in capital equipment, giving stock options to employees, acquiring smaller companies, or buying back their own stock. Fisher notes that in 1998 alone U.S. companies bought back $209 billion of their own shares instead of paying dividends. In a market downturn, however, dividend-paying companies look like firemen when you see smoke coming from your house. You want them to be there because they offer a bit of security.

The Security Blanket

The most compelling logic for a dividend is that it offers a stream of earnings that can be converted into cash payments for you, the investor. Companies without earnings can't pay a dividend and their share prices are the first to fall and take the biggest hits overall. A dividend is a tiny insurance policy and makes dividend payers competitive against bonds. As such, a dividend boosts total return, which you may recall is capital appreciation (increase in market value) plus income (the dividend). When the bear market starts to growl, the more conservative institutional investors dump their speculative holdings in favor of the consistent dividend payers because they know in a downturn they will at least get that dividend.

Given the choice between capital appreciation and a dividend, in times when corporate earnings and the economy are growing across the board, pick a company that provides the appreciation. When earnings turn flat and the economy heads south, having dividend payers is like having a security blanket. There is also a subtle relationship between dividend payers and the pure-growth companies that dominated the 1990s.

For years, the stodgy dividend payers were seen as behind the times and their stock prices languished. Old stalwarts that dominated the food, financial, utilities, and energy industries were neglected in favor of "I gotta have it" technology companies. As a result, share prices for entire out-of-favor industries were undervalued. Enter the value managers, scooping up perfectly profitable companies that the rest of the Viagra-besotted market ignored. When earnings evaporated for the techs and dot.coms, the big bananas running institutional and mutual funds did *sector rotations* into the dividend payers. That means they dumped the glamour boys and went elsewhere. Once wallflowers, the neglected dowagers became princesses in a growling market. So dividend payers were part of a move to value. They had earnings and were willing to share them when so many earnings reports were disappointing so many. That's one of the reasons why the Wilshire Value Index was only off 0.7 percent when the Wilshire Large Growth Index was being clobbered 42 percent from the March 2000 market peak sixteen months earlier. Dividend yields rise as part of the equation when stock prices fall. Higher-dividend companies qualify most of the time as being out of favor, so they are natural candidates for any value or income investor.

When you consider the handful of predictions in chapters 1 and 2—that the average returns for stocks will be in the *single* digits unless a high growth period returns—dividends become as important as trunks on elephants in achieving an inflation-beating total return. No less than Jeremy Siegel of the Wharton School of Finance pronounced in the summer of 2001 that "in the future, I believe that more attention will be paid to dividends and current earnings and less to growth."

Does the dividend yield of a stock signal a good time to buy and sell? Not really. According to Thomas Saler in *Taming the Bear: How to Invest in Stocks without Getting Eaten Alive* (Globe Pequot, 1994), "by itself the dividend yield on stocks tells you little about when to sell and even less about when to buy."

If You're In for a Penny, You're In for a Dollar

The key to building your own portfolio—even in bear markets—is consistency. If you are confident in your research, then keep buying the companies you like. Dollar-cost averaging is one of the best techniques to keep your portfolio growing. Although it's contrary to human nature to buy stock when the price is down, that's the best time to lower your average cost per share—and ultimately boost your profit when you sell. This technique also works with mutual funds, but to make it work, you have to do it on a regular basis—every paycheck, monthly or quarterly.

In a bear market, you automatically become a value investor. You are buying when others are selling, just like some of the top professional managers you've met in previous chapters. While it flies in the face of logic to buy during major market declines, that's when you'll find the greatest bargains. If you've done your homework, the rebound will be especially sweet.

DRIP Resources

There are several excellent sources of information for DRIP investors.

- George Fisher's newsletter *Power Investing with DRIPs* (www.powerinvestdrips.com; 847-446-4406) employs a comprehensive approach, but it's pricey for the average investor at $99 annually. A better value is his book *All about DRIPs and DSPs* (McGraw-Hill, $16.95), which lays out his DRIP strategy in colorful detail.

- The most complete set of DRIP resources is from Charles Carlson at Horizon Publishing (www.dripinvestor.com; 219-852-3220). Horizon publishes *The DRIP Investor,* a newsletter that follows both DIPs and DRIP plans and recommends portfolios. The newsletter, also $99 a year, has a wealth of information on the subject and updates changes in plans and suggested portfolios. Carlson has also penned several books on the subject, the most notable being *Buying Stocks without a Broker* (McGraw-Hill, 1999).

- Another useful resource is from Temper of the Times Publications (www.directinvesting.com; 800-295-2550), which also publishes *The Moneypaper, Direct Investing,* and *The DRP Authority* newsletters. Its Temper Enrollment Service features access to one thousand DRIP plans.

- Members of the American Association of Individual Investors (www.aaii.com) receive an annual issue of their *AAII Journal* that contains an extensive list of available DRIPs. Their Web site also has a generous number of articles on investing using a dividend-focused strategy.

- Another long-standing favorite among dividend-savvy investors is Geraldine Weiss's *Investment Quality Trends* newsletter (www.iqtrends.com; 858-459-3818), which tracks a number of stocks that she recommends. She's also the coauthor of *The Dividend Connection* (Dearborn Financial, $24.95), which, while out of a date, is a good starting point for learning about the subject.

- The National Association of Investors Corporation (www.better-investing.org) is the non-profit mother ship for investment clubs and features two low-cost DRIP programs, from which you can enroll in DRIP stocks if you are a member. You can join as an individual or as a club.

- In the library, consult *Moody's Handbook of Dividend Achievers, Standard & Poor's Industry Reports,* and *The Value Line Investment Survey.* All contain extensive information on earnings, predictions, company ratings, and dividend history.

There are more detailed resources in the back of the book on these organizations.

If History Is Any Judge, Dividends Will Rise Again

As I write this in late 2001, the S&P 500 dividend yield is a meager 1.3 percent. Historically, stocks have yielded close to 4 percent over most of the past century. While you can't argue that Congress will turn back the clock to favor tax treatment of dividends, in a low-return environment stocks with dividends are more attractive than those without dividends— they simply have to compete with bonds. Investors will continue to reward stocks that take more risks to produce higher returns. That much is a given. Dividends, however, serve as a way of tempering risk if you're not willing to make huge sacrifices for the return.

No matter how Uncle Sam or Wall Street sees it, there is something virtuous about a dividend. It's a reward for holding a stock. The longer you hold a stock, the more dividends—and dividend increases—you will receive (if the company stays healthy). In that light, dividends are about saving and reinvesting profits, the essence of thrift. On that subject, I know of few wittier experts than Richard Saunders, the "Poor Richard" of Ben Franklin's *Poor Richard's Almanack*. Here's one of Franklin's thoughts on thrift as rendered by Poor Dick:

> ### How to Get Riches
> The Art of getting Riches consists
> very much in Thrift. All men are not equally
> qualified for getting money, but it is in the power
> of every one alike to practice this virtue.
> He that would be beforehand in the World,
> must be beforehand with his business:
> it is not only ill Management, but discovers a slothful
> Disposition, to do that in the afternoon,
> which should be done in the morning.
> Useful attainments in your minority
> will procure riches in maturity, of which
> Writing and accounts are not of the moment.

Or, as Franklin opined in another edition of his sage almanac, "there are three faithful friends—an old wife, an old dog and ready money." Steady dividends also count when you need to restore your faith in capitalism.

CHAPTER 9

Buying into Long-Term Trends and Holding On for Dear Life

The art of living resembles wrestling more than dancing, for here a man does not know his movement and his measures before-hand. No, he is obliged to stand strong against chance, and secure himself as occasion shall offer.

—Marcus Aurelius

"It's not that I'm competitive, I'm focused." The words burst from Sam Isaly's mouth like pellets from a shotgun. Even though he is uncomfortable after a flight from London to Chicago, his persistent smile is borne of the confidence of managing money well and being right when others are wrong. Running the $1 billion-plus Eaton Vance Worldwide Health Sciences Fund, one of the top health sciences stock funds over the past three years, you have to be focused. Even with his "A-list" education, Isaly knows that he has to put up numbers every year in his business. Armed with a degree from Princeton, where one of his professors was Burton Malkiel, author of *A Random Walk Down Wall Street*, and an M.S. in economics from the London School of Economics, Isaly's business is to know the world health-care scene—and buy risk-laden stocks that may not pay off for several years.

Working as a pharmaceutical and international investment specialist for the past thirty years, Isaly looks for biotech, pharmaceutical, and health-care industry stocks from Tokyo to Tel Aviv. Like most top fund managers, he is either on the plane or on the phone and requires that his staff meet on Sunday afternoons when there are no distractions. Isaly's competitive nature is such that he revels in what his competitors own—and his fund *doesn't*—because he believes he has a good sense of what's overvalued and what's not.

Isaly's "sector" fund, which only invests in the health-care industry and related businesses, is to diversified index funds what Antarctica is to Zimbabwe. His fund only holds from forty to fifty stocks, compared to hundreds for the average index fund. He makes a few investments and hopes to beat the market, which he thrashed in 2000 with an 81.56 percent return. Except for 1995, when the fund was up 61 percent, last year was more the exception than the rule. The long-term record of the fund, however, has bested some 80 percent of the competition and averaged 22.58 percent a year over the past five years, beating the S&P 500 by nearly 9 percent and the broader Wilshire 5000 by nearly 11 percent, according to Morningstar. Through October 30, 2001, it was the third best-performing fund out of one thousand funds rated by Lipper Analytical services.

Although Isaly's fund is incredibly volatile and definitely not for nervous nellies—it has a standard deviation of 40.87—it is less risky with a fund beta of 0.66 than owning the S&P 500 (1.00 being the average of the index). When you look at the fund's holdings, you see nearly all of the big "pharmas"—Pfizer, Novartis, Lilly, Abbott, American Home Products, Pharmacia, and Schering-Plough. These large-cap drugmakers account for nearly one-third of the portfolio and add stability to the remaining holdings, which are "emerging" biotech and pharmaceutical companies that are not making money yet (about one-third of Isaly's total portfolio).

Since he invests in some of the riskiest startups in an as-yet-unproven business, biotech, Isaly controls his risk exposure by investing no more than 5 percent in each company. For the smaller companies, he is generally under 4 percent per stock. Brand-new companies are allocated no more than a 1 percent stake.

"Our moderate position size is appropriate to the risk we take.

We know the smaller companies can go up ten times in value, but they are no more than a 5 percent position. Since we assign about four 'names' (companies) per analyst (there are twelve), we have one of the lowest holdings-to-analyst ratios in the business."

By assigning fewer stocks to his analysts, who act as stock pickers, researchers, watchdogs, and champions of the stocks they monitor, Isaly can keep a better eye on the companies he owns, many of which are still shooting for their first blockbuster drug. All told, Isaly estimates his portfolio consists of 50 percent established companies and 50 percent new companies. If an analyst suggests a company to buy, Isaly makes them sell a company. "You have to fight for space in the portfolio." Isaly's research team is set up to buy companies with promising products. Not only are they picking the Mercks and Pfizers of tomorrow, they need to know when the companies will be profitable.

"We need to know who's going to make money and when. We expect to have eighty profitable companies by 2004. We make most of our money if we pick a company two years before it's profitable and hang on for two years after that."

Isaly's style is like prospecting for gold, only he's surveyed every creek and valley, started digging and panning, and inspected the terrain years before the other prospectors have arrived. He grills management, consults the four analysts who hold doctoral degrees on his staff, gets on planes, and goes all over the world. When he hits paydirt, he does well. A company called Gilead that the fund owned went public at $8 and shot up to $53. He thinks it will hit $100 and plans to hold it for five to ten years. Although he sounds brash hyping the next biotech marvel, he's as far as you can get from a "pump and dump" broker. He insists he's "an investor and not a collector."

Isaly's method is rooted in knowing the companies he buys better than a bridegroom knows his bride. He doesn't want character traits, he wants amounts and dates when things are going to happen. It's like a fiancé asking his betrothed, "Sure you're going to be a corporate lawyer. When will you pass the bar and what will be your average earnings for the next ten years after taxes?"

"I want experienced management," Isaly continues without a pause in his staccato patter. "Have they done it before [made new drugs]? Are they good business people and scientists? Do they have the pedigree [education]? I get very nosy. I want names [stocks] nobody else owns. If everyone owns a company like Merck [he doesn't and is glad he doesn't], everyone performs the same."

Despite the fact that pharmas and biotechs had a stellar year in the midst of Wall Street's burst bubble—the sectors were up 30 percent and 50 percent, respectively, in 2000—Isaly still sees ample growth for these industries. Of the twenty biotech companies that are profitable, they are growing earnings 20 percent a year. It will be rocky in the interim. In 2001, Congress was pushing to provide prescription coverage to Medicare recipients, which is a huge wildcard for the pharmas. Most health-care fund managers see Medicare changes as inevitable, and largely negative in the short term, since they will force the drugmakers to give large discounts to the government and depress profits. Isaly claims that the market has "priced in" this possibility already, although it's hard to tell what will actually happen until a bill reaches the president's desk.

Keeping up with all of the advances in health care can be bewildering, but Isaly won't be left behind on important new drugs or procedures. He won't take incoming cell phone calls in the office because he doesn't want anything to interfere with his work. When he's not working, he's with his family, fishing off Cape Cod or "simply watching the wind blow in the trees" from a country house in rural Pennsylvania. Despite having more money than time to spend it, he takes the bus to work. All New York City buses can accommodate his wheelchair [he was partially paralyzed in a high school wrestling accident], and after the twenty-minute commute, he is back to thinking about "putting up numbers so high on the board [annual returns] that nobody will be able to take them down." No, he's not competitive, he's focused—like a laser beam on a diamond.

Big Themes and How You Can Invest in Them

Demographics are destiny. Or that's what a handful of futurists have been predicting over the past few years. Just look at what has happened since the end of World War II and you can get a picture of how dramatically things have changed for our species. Most Americans forget that when Franklin Roosevelt instituted Social Security in 1935, he never thought it would burden future genera-tions because most people didn't live to be sixty-five in his time. Now we have a boom in eighty-year-olds and one-hundred-year-olds; longevity and *not* outliving your nest egg have become two of the most powerful themes of the twenty-first century.

The news has been in for a long time. Life expectancies are longer. The drugs to get us there are better. Biotechnology will allow us to rewrite biology to repair organs, mend stroke damage, strike down cancer, and eliminate horrid diseases in the womb. It's

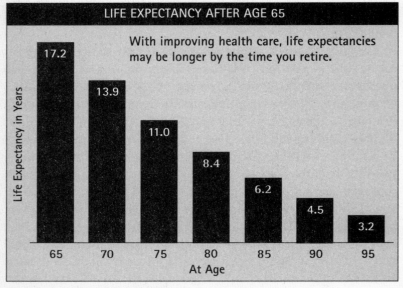

Sources: IRS and Newkirk Products, Inc.

a bit scary that we have such knowledge, but it's all in the quest of longer life and the holy grail of immortality.

Well, nobody is going to live forever, but we can enjoy the ride a bit more and make some money along the way. Sector funds shine a spotlight on health care and other industries, such as software/ electronics, financial services, energy, precious metals, regions (see chapter 7), and subsectors of industries (brokerage, insurance, medical delivery, etc.). Sector funds are popular because they allow investors to make streamlined bets on industries or parts of industries. These are not diversified funds investing across the board. They are usually betting on one race at a time with only a few horses.

When it comes to health care, an increasingly popular sector in recent years due to the growing prominence of biotechnology and drug therapies, health-care sector funds are thriving due to speculation and expectation. Speculation is a fixture of any market. Expectations can be even more troublesome since the majority of them—when it comes to stocks—are never fulfilled. There are more blind alleys in the biotech industry than mutual fund companies are willing to admit. And for every blockbuster drug, a drug company has tried some twenty thousand other compounds that didn't work. For every Prozac, Zocor, and Viagra, there are warehouses full of experiments that went nowhere.

Nevertheless, the health-care industry is built on expectations— and hope. We have come to *accept* that there will be cures for the most devastating diseases because the pharmas have a track record of delivering. Before World War II, modern antibiotics were unheard-of, there were no drugs to control cholesterol or blood pressure, and chemotherapy for cancer was practically nonexistent. And forget about chasing away depression with a pill or improving your sex life. Big bands and booze were the main drugs of the '40s. (I'll take the big bands over booze any day.)

The pressure to manufacture cures is part of the health-care establishment. Our government pours billions into universities and pharmas to find these cures. It is a part of our way of life. When we grow old, we expect Medicare to cover the cost of nearly every ailment (if you don't have insurance before then, you're out of luck). And with genomics, stem-cell research, and even more powerful computers coming on the scene, the advances in medical science over the next decades will make Arthur C. Clarke blush. In reviewing all these developments, you need to follow how demographics are changing society and what it means to you as an investor. If you can invest to take advantage of these trends, the short-term market will become irrelevant. You will make money over time and you won't care about bear markets.

- **Preventive medicine will become the prevalent form of treatment.** In many cases, preventive medicine isn't a treatment at all: It's exercise, wellness, a balanced diet, and diagnosing problems before they become life threatening. Consider that by the end of 2001, some 90 percent of insurance carriers will expand coverage or reduce premiums for those policyholders with healthy lifestyles. If you can control obesity, keep your cholesterol and blood pressure down, and exercise regularly, you have a good chance of living longer. There are a whole array of drugs, foods, and exercise regimens (health clubs) that bolster this lifestyle. It's not surprising that a Louis Harris poll found that two-thirds of those queried said they have changed their eating habits in the last five years. We want to live longer and entire industries have been created to help us do that.

- **Technology will mean more than higher productivity.** The benefits to business are obvious: doing more work faster with fewer people. Technology, however, goes beyond cell phones. Some of the biggest advances in technologies are largely unseen but making a huge impact. Energy-saving technology and fuel cells may reduce our dependence on fossil fuels. The fastest-growing energy source is the wind. There are also ways of deriving energy from the sun, the ocean, and even garbage. Every major automaker is now committed to autos that run on fuel cells or "hybrids" running on a combination of gasoline and batteries. Of course, the mainstay of technology will still be information processing and communication. By 2005, 83 percent of American management will be "knowledge workers"—people who work directly with information processing. And five of the ten fastest-growing occupations by 2005 will be computer related. Although there's a glut of processing and telecommunications capacity in 2001, the entire economy is being rebuilt around the speed of light—optical storage and transmission. In the long term, technology will be a constant and innovation will be rewarded. The future will require lots of technology, energy, and infrastructure. During the last industrial revolution, big money was made in the companies manufacturing the railroad tracks and buying the land. Today's revolution will benefit those who are laying the big information pipeline and making the switches. It's a safe bet.

▪ **Biotechnology will be to the twenty-first century what computers were to the twentieth.** I am tempted to bluster about coming cures for cancer, Parkinson's disease, Alzheimer's disease, and a host of other maladies. There will be thousands of small steps before that happens, however. Tremendous computing power is being put to work sorting out genes, proteins, and single molecules, which is a daunting process. Once this marriage is consummated, Isaly believes, "you're going to see many more therapeutic drugs hitting the market in the future, especially mid-decade and beyond."

▪ **Aging Westerners will demand more service.** I'm not referring to getting another glass of wine in a restaurant, either. Aging means more leisure time and less work; more disposable income and saving; more complex needs for services like estate planning and long-term care. The travel/tourism industry, for example, will nearly double in the next two decades. By 2020, there will be some 1.6 billion international travelers, up from 612 million in 1997, according to the World Tourism Organization. That's good news for cruise operators, airlines, travel agents, and a host of support businesses. As people age, they save more and spend less, which will benefit the huge financial sector of banks, savings and loans, brokers, financial planners, estate planners, mutual funds, and insurers. And, as people become disabled, there will be a huge need for long-term care. Around 1900, the average life expectancy was forty-six years. In 2000 it was nearly eighty years, with the eighty-five-plus age group the single fastest growing demographic group. It's a sure bet that older people will travel more, need more financial handholding, and require special housing needs. Funds and stocks that invest in these trends will do well over time.

- **The vanity business will blossom.** It already has. Plastic surgery and nutritional supplements have never been more popular. Skin improvement procedures are up 800 percent since 1990. Fitness-related products and services are growing at a steady 10 percent annual clip, notes *American Demographics.* The first wave of 77 million baby boomers (born 1946 to 1964) will be turning sixty-five in 2011 and will be doing anything they can to "keep on rocking" by staying out of the rocking chair. If it keeps you fit or purports to make you younger, the money will be spent.

- **Productivity will increase because of technology, boosting wealth.** Economists are in love with the idea of productivity, that is, working less and getting more done. Technology has made so many strides in boosting productivity that many economists insist that productivity was behind the boom years of the mid- to late 1990s. If you don't have to spend as much time at work—and your wages are at least tracking inflation—then you reap an unseen benefit. You make more money without having to work harder or longer hours. That means you'll have more money to invest and pay your bills and need the financial services to help you manage your money. Robert Davis and David Wessel explored the long-term benefits of productivity growth in *Prosperity: The Coming 20-Year Boom and What It Means to You* (Times Business, 1998):

> If the economy chugs along at 1% annual growth in productivity, the income of the typical married couple would grow from around $49,700 in 1996 to around $60,050 in 2016. Add another half-percentage point of productivity growth, and the couple would make an additional $6,000

in 2016 . . . to middle-class families, $6,000 a year is eight months' worth of mortgage payments on the typical newly purchased single-family home.

Technology puts money in your pocket indirectly, so you might as well invest in it long-term to benefit more directly.

SECTORS THAT DID WELL DURING ONE OF WALL STREET'S WORST WEEKS

Sector	Change*
Precious metals	10.11%
Water utilities	8.10%
Wireless communications	4.12%
Telecommunications	3.26%
Fixed-line comunications[†]	3.15%

*Returns reflect broad sectors for the week ending 9/21/01. While these sectors reflected Wall Street's short-term ideas of safe havens, all but precious metals could be considered worthwhile long-term investments based on growth in those sectors. [†]Fixed-line communications represent telephone companies ranging from the long-distance carriers to the regional operating phone companies. *Source:* cbsmarketwatch.com.

The following list doesn't represent my endorsement of any particular stock or mutual fund type. I've picked a few notable leaders in each category and types of sector funds that cater to them. It would be unwise to place the majority of your money in any one sector, since the demographic changes in society are going to impact *every* sector, although at different times. For most investors, you would get a piece of nearly every major sector by investing in an S&P 500 Index Fund at a fraction of the cost of investing in a sector fund (see next chapter). If that's the case, then why invest in a sector fund at all?

MATCHING SECTOR FUNDS AND STOCKS TO TRENDS

As an investor, there are ways to target these trends through stocks and mutual funds. The following matrix will show how specific funds and stocks will help you profit from these trends:

Trend	Stocks	Sector Funds
Health care	Pfizer, Merck, Pharmacia	Health care, Biotech
Medical devices	Biomet, Johnson & Johnson	Health care
Biotechnology	Amgen, Celera, Genentech	Biotech
Financial services	Citicorp, Schwab, AIG	Financial services
Housing	Del Webb, Centex, Manor Care	Real estate, REITs
Leisure and travel	American Air, Carnival, Harrah's	Leisure
Technology	Microsoft, ADC Telecom, IBM	Technology, software
Entertainment	Disney, Viacom, AOL Time Warner	Media/broadcast

Rotation Nastiness: Avoiding the Cinderella Cycles in Sectors

Long-term changes in society and the economy are in progress, although we can't see them day to day. There are more drugs coming on the market from the biotechnology boom. More housing is being tailored to those who are empty-nesters, nearly retired, fully retired, and disabled. And every industry knows where their customers are coming from and where they are headed. Harry Dent, for example, found that when people hit their peak spending years (typically at age forty-seven), they trigger a boom in all kinds of consumer spending, from appliances to mutual funds. And these consumers indirectly benefit the stock prices of specific companies in sectors where the spending is greatest.

If a diversified mutual fund will give you decent exposure to profit from all of these developments, why concentrate your money on a few dozen companies at a time? The answer is in an obscure phrase mentioned earlier: *sector rotation*.

When money managers conclude—often in a herdlike fashion—that certain sectors are "overbought" (read: time to take profits and sell), they usually reinvest that money elsewhere. If stocks are generally dour, they buy bonds or sit in cash. Stock-fund managers generally are obligated to find other stocks that are either growing earnings or are bargains (depending on whether they have a growth or value orientation, or both). That's when they head to a sector where the p/e's and prices are lower.

Back to the supermarket analogy. If you want peaches and they are sold out, out of season, or selling for $10 a pound, you look at the price of bananas, pears, or apples. The same thing happens in the stock market. During a prolonged sell-off or correction phase, money managers buy stocks with reasonable prices, high probabilities of posting profits, and dividends to boost returns in a sagging market. When technology shares lost their "Cinderella" status in 2000, the big money went over to health-care stocks, snapping up dividend-rich pharmas and some sturdy biotechs. In 2001, when those stocks fell out of favor, some money floated into energy, utilities, and food companies. Then financial services were the favorite sons. And so it goes, with fast money always chasing the highest returns.

Sometimes a sector is only in favor for a few months. Often it's a few years, which is what happened to technology. Every sector has its day in the sun. Even precious metals, which are lousy investments in a low-inflation environment, shine when there's a sniff of inflation. Sector rotation is a nasty reality in both the stock and bond markets. Managers are always seeking "quality" (read: a sure way to make money when other sectors aren't) and will trash one sector to go to another like an angry two-year-old grabbing his marbles and going home.

The most dramatic example of sector rotation was seen in technology stocks. In 1999, technology issues were the best-performing sector, ringing up a 76.9 percent gain. The following year, the tide went out and tech stocks lost 34.1 percent. Cinderella turned into a smashed pumpkin in the course of a year.

The only way not to get hurt by the fickle nastiness of sector rotation and Cinderella cycles is to invest in sectors long term and to diversify as much as possible. It's okay to concentrate a small portion of your money (not more than 20 percent) on a handful of sectors. You'll probably do well over time. But you have to stay with it through the down years to reap the benefits of the up years. Sectors in the short term are the riskiest, most volatile forms of investing. Don't put your money in them unless you have decades to invest your money and you understand that, as a long-term investor, you know that most of the investments within these funds won't pan out. *Fund managers may hit a few winners or have several off years. If you can't tolerate that kind of risk, don't even think about sector funds.*

Don't Do What Most People Do: Invest High and Sell Low

This sounds counterintuitive, I know. I've done it myself more than once because I wasn't paying attention to my long-term goals in a fund. Most of the money in sector funds comes in and leaves at the wrong time—consistently. Remember the halcyon years of technology funds, when stocks like Cisco, Microsoft, and Oracle simply couldn't miss? Let me refresh your memories of the good old days.

During 1998, technology-stock mutual funds soared 53.9 percent. In 1999, they added a heart-pounding 136.6 percent and another 19.1 percent during the first three months of 2001. More than half of the $167 billion in tech funds came in the *last six months* of the ride of the Valkyries before the gates of Valhalla slammed shut in March 2001. And that's fairly typical if you look at mutual-fund money flows in previous sector-fund bubbles, notes the *Wall Street Journal*.

In 1991, health-care and biotech funds were in the spotlight, quadrupling assets after a run-up of 63.8 percent. The performance of these funds was subpar the following year and the hot money fled again. I call this the "bigger jackpot effect," which I noted in the opening section of my last book, *The Kitchen-Table Investor*. When the total prize goes up, players think they have a *better* chance of winning and start playing the game in hordes. It's a casino mentality. Hot-performing funds rarely have two great years in a row, but the jackpot effect suspends logic. This happens every time a state lottery jackpot goes up. More people play even though the odds of winning are still 10 million to one. The odds of winning don't recede because more money is in the kitty.

Money that came late to the game in the late '90s tech run-up mostly bailed when the market turned south and institutional managers sold anything with "technology," "telecommunications," or "Internet" in the title. The majority of investors who bought high sold low. The fund companies do everything to encourage this behavior by launching sector funds at the height of a sector's popularity. So investors buy high and ultimately sell low as a way of cutting their losses, although what they do is *guarantee* their losses.

Some of the more responsible fund companies add disincentives for selling out of sector funds ("redemptions" in trade paralance), like tagging on additional fees if you sell less than a year after you buy or raising account minimums to $25,000. Still, with nearly four hundred sector funds to choose from, it's all too tempting to chase last year's returns in the hot sector du jour.

Another compelling reason to avoid sector funds is that they are expensive to operate and the costs are passed along to you, the shareholder. The annual range of expenses deducted from your assets by management is 0.34 percent to 2.44 percent annually, 1.72 percent being the average. Add to that a sales charge with some funds and you have an expensive enterprise if you are losing money.

I cannot recommend that you put more than 20 percent of your money in a sector fund or hold it for fewer than ten years. If you can't stay the course to see a trend play out in the marketplace, then stay away from these vehicles. Because you are concentrating your risk in one small part of the world economy, sector funds should only be owned if you have a diversified portfolio across the board: large-cap growth and value; mid- and small-cap growth and value; bonds; real estate; and cash. In the short term they are a form of gambling but if you are serious about holding sector funds long term they are strong investments.

TOP SECTOR FUNDS

Fund	5-year Return	Phone
Biotech and health care		
Dresdner RCM Biotech N	40.21%*	(800) 726-7240
Eaton Vance Worldwide Health†	22.27%	(800) 225-6265
Vanguard Health Care	23.19%	(800) 662-7447
Energy		
Fidelity Select Energy‡	5.80%	(800) 544-8888
Invesco Energy Inv.	7.36%	(800) 525-8085
Vanguard Energy	5.69%	(800) 662-7447
Financial services		
Century Shares Trust	17.07%	(800) 321-1928
Fidelity Select Financial Services‡	13.77%	(800) 544-8888
Invesco Financial Services Inv.	13.23%	(800) 525-8085
Miscellaneous		
Fidelity Utilities*	7.59%	(800) 544-8888
Invesco Leisure Inv.	21.03%*	(800) 525-8085
T. Rowe Price Media & Telecom	17.14%	(800) 231-8432
Technology		
Fidelity Select Electronics‡	19.99%	(800) 544-8888
Firsthand Tech Value‡	14.22%	(800) 884-2675
Invesco Technology Inv.	8.14%	(800) 525-8085

*Fund started in 1997; three-year return only. †5.75% maximum sales charge. ‡Carries redemption fee. Period ending 12/31/01. *Source:* Morningstar.

A Cautionary Tale: Mea Culpa

I can attest to the dangers of sector funds because my wife and I succumbed to their deadly charms and lost money over the last few years. Distracted by any number of other things (okay, it's an excuse), I managed to switch my wife's SEP-IRA money into health-care and technology sector funds, which I also held in my SEP-IRAs. To compound this crazy antidiversification scheme, I was chasing the technology boom through my 401(k) account, which was 60 percent invested in the technology-crazy Janus Twenty Fund. So we got burned and my wife went nuts every time she got a quarterly statement, so we switched into diversified value and growth funds. I maintain my position in a health-care fund (The Vanguard Health Care Fund), because I'm going to leave it alone in my Roth IRA for the next few decades.

Sector funds have this tendency to show you the possibilities of extreme profits in a narrowly focused portfolio, and then pull the rug from under you just when you've made a decision to buy. And there are more cautionary tales out there than mine. In late 2001, the ProFunds Internet Fund was down a numbing 90 percent for the year, followed by the Jacob Internet Fund, which was down 79.4 percent. And these funds have plenty of company. Would you feel comfortable looking at your fund statement, knowing that only 10 percent to 20 percent of your money was left? These funds may or may not rebound, but you need to know that they offer no protection when sector rotation turns against you. They are all-or-nothing propositions.

. . .

There's a fable about all-or-nothingness that I'd like to share with you. A fisherman once lived in a ramshackle cottage by the sea with his wife. He was fishing for days with nothing to show for his time when he felt a tug at his line. When he hauled up the fish, it was a flounder who began to talk to him. "I beg you not to kill me, for I am really an enchanted prince, so please let me go!" The fisherman obliged and returned to his wife to tell her about his incredible day.

"So let me get this straight," says the wife. "You catch this enchanted talking fish and you don't even ask for a wish before you throw him back? Get your butt back in that boat. Ask him if he can get us out of this stinking hole and into better digs! Talk to the fish, or I'm out of here."

The man returned to the sea reluctantly and set his line in the water. After many frustrating hours, he yelled out to the fish to come up, and the fish surfaced.

"Sorry to bother you, prince," the fisherman said, "but my wife was wondering how she could get a nice house."

"Go back to your new home," the fish said, and swam away.

The man went home again, and was astounded to find that in its place was a lovely ranch home with a wide porch, two-car garage, and plenty of storage for his fishing equipment. His wife gave him the tour of the new master bath and bedroom, the powder room, and a kitchen filled with new appliances. After a week, however, the wife grew restless.

"Husband, you know that if the fish can produce a house like *this*, he can certainly build us a bigger house. This house doesn't have a basement or a guest room or a place for me to sew and knit. Go back and talk to your fish again, or I will divorce you."

So once again, the fisherman spent untold hours in the boat until he cried out in frustration to summon the flounder. The fish, upon hearing his wife's new request, sent the man home again.

In the place of the tidy ranch house was a ten-thousand-square-foot castle with an immense atrium, six bedrooms, a media/recreation room, exercise room/spa, and kitchen with professional-quality appliances. The home also had a five-car garage, koi pond, and a master bathroom that could accommodate a fleet of boats.

The wife was happy for another week, until she started pining for a country club membership, a winter home in Maui, a new wardrobe, a trip around the world, a sports car, SUV, luxury sedan, a boat of her own, a portfolio of technology stocks, and enough money so that she could knock down her new home and build the largest custom home possible.

Shocked at his wife's avarice, the fisherman reluctantly said he would return to the fish, but was unsure of what the fish would say. An angry storm was raging and the fisherman was unable to put his boat into the boiling waves. He shouted in desperation. The fish floated close to shore and listened to the man once more.

"Now what does she want?" the fish asked derisively.

"She wants to be a master of the universe," the fisherman said with a mixture of sarcasm and truth.

"Then she shall have her cottage again. Go home, she is waiting for you there."

Markets have a way of humbling us if we seek too much. There's nothing wrong with merging our need for growth with a little risk taking, but you have to balance that risk carefully.

CHAPTER 10

The Route to Simplicity:
Index Funds Balance Costs
and Boost Returns

Investment management is a field fraught with fragility and fallibility, a field in which today's careful, rational fund selections are too often tomorrow's embarrassments.

—John Bogle

The idea that you can outperform a market average more than once is like thinking you're going to find a talking flounder. If it does happen—and you get cocky—you will eventually sink back to below-average status. For most investors, the intangible truth is that everyone would like to beat the market, but few ever do, and not because of personality or intellect. As a group, investors represent the entire market, according to modern portfolio theory; therefore it's not possible to beat the market over long stretches of time.

You can get lucky and go against the grain. Pick an out-of-favor sector that rebounds. That takes guts and a bit of pluck, and most people don't like to take those kinds of risks unless they are being paid by someone else to run money. There are so many ways of getting it wrong that even the smartest of investors fail miserably at market timing the way most golfers fail to get close to a hole in one.

Carlton Martin is paid to either stay near or beat the market average. As the manager of the $700 million TIAA-CREF Growth & Income Fund, he's trying to get a slightly above-average return through what is called an "enhanced index/active approach." This style of "dual investment management strategy" places the bulk of the fund's assets in the S&P 500 Index. Martin is doing what most of us need to be doing with our portfolios and what most of us *want* to be doing. By aiming for the average return of the S&P 500—and then "enhancing" that return by actively managing a portion of the portfolio—Martin is trying to put a little spin on the ball to reap better returns. The avid jogger and golfer has fulfilled that part of his charter, averaging 20.5 percent annual return over the past three years, compared to 17.63 percent for the competing Vanguard S&P 500 Fund. Since inception, the fund returned an average 8.31 percent (from September 2, 1997, to December 31, 2000).

With an undergraduate degree in accounting and banking experience, neither field appealed to the Jamaican-born Martin, who obtained his MBA from American University in 1972, at the beginning of a miserable period for stock investors. He thought about becoming a credit officer for the World Bank, but took a job with TIAA-CREF in 1980 and discovered that the intellectual challenge of analyzing stocks was engaging and addictive.

Martin has the flexibility to go stock picking when he sees opportunities. The passive portion of his portfolio is about 50 percent to 60 percent of total assets, leaving him 40 percent to 50 percent to invest as he sees fit. Typical index funds have 100 percent of their portfolios as fixed investments in the stocks representing an index. The popular S&P 500 Index, for example, has stocks representing five hundred of the largest companies listed on the New York Stock Exchange. The Wilshire 5000, also referred to as "the total market," represents most of the stocks listed on all of the major exchanges, so it's the broadest possible market index. There are also indexes representing small-cap, mid-cap, value, and international funds, plus bonds and REITs.

The main virtue of an index fund is that it's destined to beat most actively managed mutual funds over time because the *costs of operation are lower* than actively managed funds. The holdings of index funds are almost never sold (unless a stock or two drops out of the index), so there are virtually no management and transactions costs. Because there's no *turnover*—the buying and selling of securities—the fund managers don't have to pay commissions (and charge shareholders), lowering a fund's *expense ratio*. This percentage is the annual amount of money a fund manager deducts from assets every year to cover the costs of running the fund. An annual expense ratio of 1.5 percent a year is outrageous in the world of index funds, where the big index funds can be run for as little as 0.20 percent a year. Whatever you pay a fund manager out of your own money reduces your total return, so the lower the expense ratio, the better. (Martin's fund weighs in at 0.43 percent, mostly due to a waiver of 0.50 percent of management fees until 2006.)

Although his fund suffered with the rest of the pack in 2000 (down 7.3 percent), Martin posted good numbers in 1998 and 1999, beating the S&P 500 in each of those years. Despite TIAA-CREF's mission to manage $270 billion for 2 million employees at eleven thousand colleges and related institutions, Martin has a fair amount of latitude to work with his portfolio and the twenty-four analysts who support it.

"We are completely opportunity driven," Martin says of the active part of his portfolio. "We have a combination of growth and value and we tilt toward large-cap growth and large-cap value. In picking out stocks, we try to find pricing anomalies [where the stock price doesn't reflect the company's value]. We have found that more than 40 percent of the companies out there are mispriced."

Martin's blended approach allows him to look at larger demographic trends and companies that are well-managed but bargain-priced. He won't let a single company comprise more than 5 percent of his portfolio, which is a common risk-reduction technique. He also keeps an eye on specific sectors like technology and health care to make sure that he's weighing their risk to reward ratios appropriately. That helps buttress the portfolio against sector rotation, although he got stung in 2001 by some of his technology holdings.

Another risk management technique is the portfolio's require-ment that it hold at least 80 percent in dividend-producing stocks. The dividend yield of the portfolio is slightly below that of the S&P 500 Index (0.8 percent as this goes to press), but it's more than what one would find in an all-technology sector fund. Along the way, he may pick up some battered, well-managed technology companies and add to his pharmaceutical company holdings. He sees a rebound in technology and is confident that aging baby boomers will support the growth of pharmas for years to come. All told, the fund's turnover is some 20 percent to 30 percent a year with the average holding period of his stocks from three to five years.

"When I talk with my analysts, we discuss the market landscape and the beneficiaries within that landscape. Who will benefit and add value? We don't want to trade in and out of stocks. We need a long-term thesis and perspective. We look at an 18-month time frame initially and look for leaders [in specific industries] at attrac-tive valuations [prices]."

Investing in companies that "benefit and improve the quality of life," Carlton's fund has a socially responsible perspective as part of one of the largest pension systems in the world. He also has the luxury of keeping long-term investors, who typically don't with-draw their money when the market turns ugly. TIAA-CREF investors also make biweekly contributions, so he has a steady flow of cash to invest. Like the value managers, he's always interested in "companies that have an ability to generate cash flow in the future." Following the average of S&P 500 stocks, he tries to match the p/e's and earnings growth of the broad index while scouting around the world for stocks that might beat it.

It's difficult to say whether Martin's "dual management invest-ment strategy" will succeed over time. The odds are that he will somewhat keep pace with the S&P 500, although never consis-tently beating it over any ten-year period. The combination of

dividend-paying growth stocks, some value picks, small companies, and foreign securities (up to 20 percent) is a sensible combination to allay volatility concerns. This is certainly not the most
conservative approach, nor is it daring like a sector fund. It will
have the volatility of the broad market while keeping in mind Martin's suggestion that those committed to the stock market "be able
to sleep at night knowing there will be some volatility."

Martin's synthesis of a standard index approach—and the low
operating costs—with some active stock picking is a workable
model for most investors with an eye on risk. It won't sacrifice too
much return, however, as it has some reasonable safeguards built in
for long-term investors.

Why Costs Matter: John Bogle's Bagel

Carlton Martin gives us a point of departure to meet John Bogle,
who has been at the epicenter of index-fund investing for the past
quarter century. When you see the gaunt, distinguished Bogle
speak, you realize that he's more than the godfather of index funds.
He's a truth teller who often berates the mutual-fund and money-
management industries. Having received a heart transplant a few
years ago, he is as vigorous as ever, and continues to staunchly
defend the idea that investing generally costs the investor too
much. The former chairman of the $570 billion Vanguard Group,
the second-largest mutual fund manager on the planet (behind
$896 billion Fidelity Investments), Bogle has been in the business
for fifty years and can document how his business evolved in stunning detail.

Despite his position as a leader in an industry that makes nearly
a penny and a half on every dollar put in a stock mutual fund,
Bogle's resonant baritone voice is revered by the individual
investors who mob him after every speech. He clearly tries to represent the little guy against a $6.8 trillion industry. Of the several
times I've heard Bogle address the Morningstar mutual funds conference (I've attended every conference from its inception through
2001), the rooms in which he speaks are as quiet as funeral homes.

Not every money manager in the room wants to hear his message, although everyone from a hotshot sector manager to the guy refilling the water carafe is listening raptly.

Playing on a William Safire metaphor, Bogle once called the index fund a "bagel." It's hard and crusty, not always the first choice for breakfast. More often than not, however, Bogle says the industry serves up "doughnuts," managed funds of all stripes that attempt to beat the index. Most doughnuts are sweet confections and offer empty calories in the Bogle lexicon. They fail to match the power and durability of the proverbial bagel. The failure of doughnutlike funds is predicated on the returns of the indexes, which beat nearly every money manager over time.

On the one hand, the indexes represent benchmarks of a cornucopia of securities. In an index, you have diversification, a little yield, and the average of all the securities in one class. In one number, you have the market average for the kind of securities you want to depict. Large-company growth stocks are represented by the S&P 500; small-company stocks by the Russell 2000; foreign stocks by the MSCI EAFE Index. Any money manager who manages securities can be compared to the indexes. If they beat the index, they're above average, but these managers are few and far between. If they're underperforming, they're in the majority. Most managers can't beat the index consistently. Comparing managers to indexes is a universal standard in the business today.

The indexes also allow you to compare how your manager did by specific asset class. For example, say you have a mid-cap stock fund. There's an S&P Midcap Index to use as a benchmark. How about long-term government bonds, European stocks, or even mortgage securities? There are indexes for all of those assets. There's a clear measure of objectivity with indexes because the companies maintaining the indexes don't have anything to do with the majority of mutual funds or money managers. Standard & Poor's, for example, is owned by McGraw-Hill, which publishes *Business Week, Moody's Investors Guides*, and thousands of business books. The question with any mutual fund, partly thanks to Bogle, is, "Did my fund beat the index?" Most don't.

Since indexes began to be used to judge the performances of money managers, the business has not been the same. When a money manager brags that "I'm returning twelve percent a year," it means little until you compare it to an index that measures the kinds of stocks he's managing. If the S&P 500 is returning 17 percent a year, he has an empty boast. He's underperforming the market index. You'd be better off in an S&P 500 index fund charging you 0.20 percent a year rather than pay this guy 2 percent a year to produce below-average returns. You can make more money and add simplicity to your portfolio with one move.

When John Bogle launched the S&P 500 fund for Vanguard more than twenty-five years ago, the investment community was amused. How dare this guy compare us to some obscure index, they chortled. The Dow Jones Industrial Average (DJIA) was the master barometer of the times, even though it only tracked the performance of thirty large industrial stocks, leaving whole industries unrepresented. As old habits die hard, even today most news organizations routinely and mistakenly quote the hourly DJIA as if it were the sole proxy of what a market of more than five thousand stocks is doing. It's simply ridiculous to make such an assumption when there are so many different components of the market that can be averaged into a more holistic picture by the S&P 500, which represents a much larger cross-section of corporate America—75 percent of stocks by capitalization—or the Wilshire 5000, which gives you the big picture.

Vanguard's index funds grew over the years as Bogle kept expanding his offerings to track all kinds of stocks *and* bonds. The rest of the industry watched and waited until they saw Vanguard raking in some real money in the 1990s—-Vanguard reaped $187 million from its fees on the S&P 500 Fund in 2000 alone. Bereft of ways to beat the market index on their own, the major fund and brokerage houses started to copy Bogle, who was able to run Vanguard funds "at cost." The industry saw that not only were investors learning about the benefits of index investing, they were making money by eschewing active managers who were turning over their portfolios at a rapid clip and charging people for the privilege of underperforming the index. Astute investors wised up and saw their money being wasted for no particular reason other than obeying the ego-space myth that they, too, could beat the market with active management.

Of the more than eight thousand mutual funds on the market, costs declined on average across the board in the 1990s. Whether Bogle spurred this development or the industry simply had better economies of scale and passed along savings to shareholders, industry watchers will be debating for a long time. Bogle certainly gained an Olympian influence over this fifty-year career in the business. He used his public appearances and many writings to herald the virtues of curtailing costs and indexing. The following chart from the Investment Company Institute, the trade organization representing the mutual fund industry, tells some of the story of the reduction in costs.

THE BOGLE FACTOR?
MUTUAL FUND COSTS DECLINE OVER TIME

Fund	1990 Average Cost	1998 Average Cost	Cost Down
Stock funds	1.81%	1.35%	35%
Bond funds	1.71%	1.09%	36%
Money-market funds	0.53%	0.42%	21%

Costs = sales-weighted average of total shareholder costs for individual funds. *Source: ICI Mutual Fund Factbook.*

I have a fairly certain feeling that Bogle would find the previous table appalling since he would argue that fund groups haven't lowered their expenses *enough* and some of the management fees they charge are still usurious. Bogle, however, is in a good position to say he practiced what he preached. A study done by Kanon Bloch Carré, a New York–based investment research and management firm, found that Vanguard's weighted expense ratio was the lowest of the top five fund groups and 5,140 funds surveyed. Here's how the study rated the top five mutual fund houses, which represent 50 percent of all mutual fund assets:

EXPENSES: A SNAPSHOT OF THE BIG FIVE FUND HOUSES

Fund Company	Assets ($ in billions)	Expense Ratio*
Vanguard	$344	0.27%
Capital Research	$203	0.62%
Fidelity	$450	0.67%
Janus	$126	0.86%
Putnam	$151	0.89%
Study Average		1.44%

*Weighted expense ratio of 5,140 stock funds through 12/31/00. *Source:* Kanon Bloch Carré, www.kanon.com.

Although these numbers don't seem very large, consider that the spread between the lowest and highest ratios—all of which are below the overall average of this study—represents a factor of nearly 200 percent. The difference between Fidelity, the largest fund manager, and #2 Vanguard means that Fidelity is charging twice as much as Vanguard to manage stock funds.

HOW INDEXING WORKS

There are two ways an index can track a basket of stocks, bonds, or REITs. The *replication* method buys stocks or bonds in similar proportions to the index itself. Let's say, for the sake of argument, that GE represents 1% of the S&P 500. An index fund using the replication method would invest 1% of its assets in GE. Another method is the *sampling* method, which is often employed for bond funds. Using a computer program, managers identify a representative sample of securities to buy that will mimic the index. That way, the index fund has a representative sample of the securities in the index without having to own every security. Index fund managers often have the freedom to invest in securities outside the index to raise potential returns and lower potential risk.

These figures, of course, are like looking at a herd of beef cattle and trying to guess how much each cow weighs. They are meaningless unless you look at the relationship between costs and returns. In no way can you interpret this study as a blanket endorsement for Vanguard, since it manages so much money in many different channels and each fund performs differently. To

HOW EXPENSES CAN AFFECT RETURN

Different Expense Ratio, Identical Performance
Consider $10,000 investments in two funds. The first fund (A) has an expense ratio of 1.10%. The second fund (B) has an expense ratio of 1.74%. Both funds have annual returns of 10% a year on their portfolios before taking fees into account. The investment in the fund with the lower expense ratio would grow to $302,771 in 40 years. The investment in the second fund would grow to $239,177, or $63,594 less than the first fund.

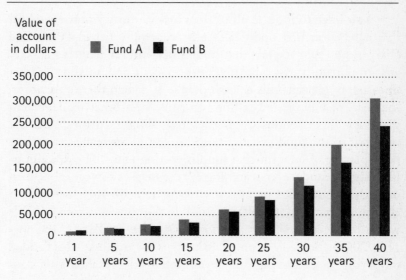

| Fund A | Expense ratio of 1.10% |
| Fund B | Expense ratio of 1.74% |

Initial investment in each fund is $10,000

Source: Investment Company Institute.

understand how costs impact performance, you need to understand the hole that money flows into if you're an unsuspecting investor.

Why Costs Matter: The Doughnut Hole

You don't have to agree with Bogle to understand that an excessive fee on any investment is money going into a black hole. By excessive, I mean paying more than average for a mutual fund, brokerage account, or even DRIP account. Costs are critical because a money manager can provide you all the services in the world and it won't add a cent to your return. It's the doughnut hole. After you'd loaded up on the sugar and carbohydrates from that sweet little morsel, you have total emptiness. I don't want to sound nihilistic, so let's look at the record:

▪ **You have to look at all of the costs in money management.** I've barely touched upon sales fees, redemption fees (Vanguard charges these), or the fact that some stock-fund managers may create "opportunity risk" by investing in cash and missing market upturns. Bogle calls this a "cash drag." And then there's turnover, the costs of buying and selling securities, and other management expenses. Transactions costs (buying/selling securities) are not reflected in the fund expense ratio, so you never really get a complete picture of how much a fund is costing you. "The doughnut-like mutual funds, ever-searching for the market's sweet spots, turn over their portfolios at an astonishing rate of 90% per year— clearly short-term speculation, not long-term investing," Bogle writes in his epic *Bogle on Investing: The First 50 Years* (McGraw-Hill, 2000). Bogle goes on to estimate what turnover costs added to paying taxes on high-turnover funds. He reached this conclusion:

AVERAGE MUTUAL FUNDS VERSUS
THE WILSHIRE 5000 INDEX FUND: COST COMPARISONS*

Cost	Average Mutual Fund	Wilshire 5000 Fund
Average nominal return on stocks	18.0%	17.7%
Sales commission @ 6%	−0.5%	—
Cash drag	−0.6%	—
Transaction costs	−0.7%	—
Expenses (ratio)	−1.2%	−0.2%
Taxes	−2.7%	−0.9%
After-tax/expenses return	**12.3%**	**16.6%**
Reduction in return	−5.7%	−1.1%

*15 years ending 11/30/99. *Source:* Adapted from *Bogle on Investing* (McGraw-Hill, 2000).

Bogle's skewed example, which I've edited for clarity, is not a representative sample of all stock funds, nor does it fairly compare all "no-load" (no sales charge) funds or all funds with the same expense levels. His larger point is that active management will dramatically eat into your total return before you've even looked at comparing performance. That means, using Bogle's example, you could be getting a 2 percent return if stocks are returning 8 percent in an actively managed fund. Does that sound right?

I know it's hard to get hot and bothered over *not* making 4.3 percent. What if the fund manager is a solid performer? What if the manager can get close to the market index? Isn't it worth it? Suppose the manager has a great year and beats the index. It's been known to happen.

▪ **You have to consider the impact of expenses over time.** Bogle is hardly sugar-coating his message when he notes, "The typical equity fund has proven dangerous to the wealth of investors who succumbed to its sugary smiles." Then he offers up an example that hits home. Say you invested $10,000 in the average mutual fund over the past fifteen years. You would have $57,000 after a decade and a half. Then compare it to investing the same amount in the Wilshire 5000 Index; you'd have a cool $100,000. Put another way, the managed stock fund gave you 48 percent of the market's return after fees and expenses were deducted from your account over time, while the low-expense index fund gave you 87 percent of the market's return minus expenses. That's math you can't argue against.

- **Even the best money managers can't beat the index.** Every year since 1987, Morningstar awards a "manager of the year" honor to the bond and fund managers who managed to not only best their peers' performance, but beat market averages. Ever a spoilsport, Bogle looked at those managers' cumulative returns from 1987 to 1998, then compared them to the return of the S&P 500 over the same period—and their follow-up returns after their winning years. The result: the managers had a respectable annual average return of 16.2 percent compared to 24.3 percent for the index. The unmanaged index beat the hottest hands in the business by 50 percent. Most of the reason for that figure is that even the best managers can't consistently repeat their best year, much less beat the index on a regular basis. Bogle cites research that has shown that funds that "rank in the top 20 in a given year have, on average, ranked 240 (of 554 funds) in the subsequent year." That means the best funds become average performers sooner rather than later, or "regress to the mean," in the lingo of statisticians.

- **Over long periods, the index wins and managers lose.** By virtue of having to justify higher costs in the form of higher returns, managers simply can't beat the index until they *both* out-perform and donate their services. Bogle actually trumpeted in one of his speeches, "fellow indexers, be of stout heart: active managers as a group never win." Bogle looked at ten-year periods going back fifty years to see if he was right.

50 YEARS: THE ACTIVE MANAGER CAN'T BEAT THE INDEX

Period	S&P Index	Stock Funds	Difference (Between Index and Stock Funds)
50 years	13.6%	11.8%	+1.8%
40 years	12.0%	10.5%	+1.5%
30 years	12.7%	10.7%	+2.0%
20 years	17.7%	15.1%	+2.6%
10 years	19.2%	15.2%	+4.0%

Periods ending 12/31/99. *Source: Bogle on Investing: The First 50 Years.*

▪ **Expenses have an even more dramatic impact on income investments.** Because bonds and cash equivalents emphasize income and not capital appreciation, expenses eat into returns directly, and often severely. Bond funds differ little from category to category. A money-market fund is going to primarily buy bonds that mature in under a year. An intermediate-bond fund will have bonds with an average maturity of about five years. There's really little management involved. So expenses make a huge difference in total return. For my short-term savings, I recently began checking out yields on bond funds to enhance the paltry 3.1 percent return I was getting on my money-market fund. I was willing to take a little bit more risk, so I started comparing intermediate-term bond funds that invested in a combination of corporate and Treasury bonds. I found two funds I liked: A fund rated highly by all of the rating services yielding about 6.7 percent and a fund yielding about the same representing an index of intermediate bonds. The index fund had an expense ratio of 0.21 percent; the top-rated fund had an expense ratio of 1.75 percent plus a 3.75 percent sales charge. Which fund do you think I chose? As Bogle warns, "Never, never invest in a bond fund without knowing its expense ratio."

▪ **There's a powerful relationship between risk-adjusted returns and costs.** Bogle did a study in 1998 that he hoped would show the relationship of risk to costs. He published this highly readable report in *The Journal of Portfolio Management*. Although the results of the study reinforce what he had been saying for years—lower costs translate into higher returns—he found a side benefit of lower-cost investing. "The funds in the group with the lowest expense ratios have the highest net returns. At the same time, they assume a nearly identical level of risk (volatility), and therefore provide distinctly higher risk-adjusted returns. . . . Now we seem to be on to something important. *With risk astonishingly constant, high returns are directly associated with low costs* [italics his]." He further discovered that "each 1% increase in the expense ratio has, on average, reduced the net total return earned by shareholders by 1.80%." Moreover, actively managed funds tend to be more volatile than index funds. According to Morningstar, the average domestic equity fund was 15 percent more volatile than the Vanguard 500 Index Fund over the past decade. Add to that the fact that 85 percent of all large-cap index funds underperformed the S&P 500 Index over the past years and you have one of the best arguments for index funds as a "core" holding (one you needn't change for decades) in your portfolio.

- **Index funds are more tax efficient.** The largest index funds have almost no turnover, meaning they don't generate much in the way of capital gains. Compare that to turnover of actively managed

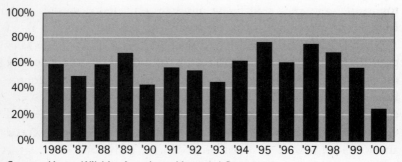

INDEXING BEATS MANAGED STOCK FUNDS MOST OF THE TIME

Percentage of diversifed U.S. stock funds that were beaten by the Wilshire 5000 Stock Index.

Sources: Lipper, Wilshire Associates, Vanguard Group.

funds—often exceeding 100 percent—and you have a formula for partially reducing your tax bill.

It All Comes Down to Risk and Return

I am not canonizing John Bogle, nor should you accept everything he says as gospel. He has been beating the drum for index funds all these years because Vanguard has been selling them and was building a market niche, which it found in a big way. And now that Bogle is no longer running the company and is free to say anything he wants about the industry (which he has throughout his career anyway), he does so with impunity and investors love it. He even has a staunch following among investors, who proudly call themselves "Bogleheads" when they leave messages on the Internet. You can't argue, however, with the fact that the vast majority of money managers can't beat a market index most of the time. It can't be done.

Burton Malkiel, the esteemed Princeton economics professor, proved the "also-ran" nature of mutual fund managers. Malkiel looked at the top 20 mutual funds from 1990 to 1994 and calculated the returns of the funds over the next five years. Over the initial four-year period, the funds managed to beat the S&P 500 Index by an average of 9.2 percent. Had you invested *only* during that period in those funds and pulled your money out and invested in U.S. Treasury bills in 1995, you would have had a good reason to be proud—and wealthier. In the next five years, however, those top funds trailed the market average by 2 percentage points a year. Malkiel found similar results in the 1980s.

It's clear that you are taking more risk by staying with a poorly performing managed fund. That's one risk that the managed mutual-fund business would prefer that you ignore. Sure, there are funds and managers that beat the index every other year. You can even go through Vanguard's large stable of funds and see scores of examples of their actively managed funds that are beating the appropriate index fund. Does that contradiction build a case for managed funds? No. In time the troll named "regression to the mean" catches up with even the best managers and they become average or less-than-average performers.

What about the years in which the indexes themselves represent overall poor returns for stocks or bonds? Can't active managers beat the indexes then by avoiding stocks heavily weighted in the indexes posting negative returns? After all, in the first half of 2001, an awful time for almost every stock index (especially those measuring large-cap growth), 59 percent of stock mutual funds were beating the S&P 500. Keep in mind, however, that these "stock pickers" are not identified. Are they primarily value-oriented funds that avoided technology stocks? Are there funds that beat the average simply by losing *less money* than the index? As Mark Twain once said, there are "lies, damn lies and statistics." In the end, we're all average. In the money management world, most are less than average over time.

BEST INDEX FUNDS

Fund	5-year Return	Phone
Best Stock Index Funds		
TIAA-CREF Growth & Income*	–1.30%*	(800) 223-1200
Vanguard 500 Index	10.06%	(800) 662-7447
Schwab Small-Cap Index Sel*	–2.16%	(800) 435-4000
Best bond index funds		
Vanguard Total Bond Index	7.76%	(800) 662-7447
Vanguard Short-Term Bond	7.11%	(800) 662-7447
Vanguard Intermediate-Term Bond	8.05%	(800) 662-7447

Period ending 12/31/01. *3-year annualized return. *Source:* Morningstar.

Nevertheless, most investors will succumb to the wisdom of the broker who calls them up and offers them the next best thing, believing the mystical incantation of someone who doesn't know any more about the market than you do. They will try to impress you with the depth of their firm's research and the thousands employed to sort out the hidden lexicon of profit.

"So the vast majority of analysts and money managers continue to put in long hours honing their analytical skills and looking for that one insight that will give them an edge," writes John Rubino in *Main Street, Not Wall Street* (Morrow, 1998). "For most professional money managers this has become an exercise in futility. And this futility has become the dirty little secret of the investment world." Indexing offers you an advantage that no single money manager can give you: as much of the market as you want at low cost.

The King and the Bishop

Although the index fund was clearly not invented in Denmark, I have a Danish fable that relates to the deception of appearances. A bishop had once written on his gates and doors, "I am the wisest man on earth." When word of this boast reached the king, he was infuriated and demanded that the bishop account for his wisdom. When the bishop visited the king and assured him that he, the bishop, was the wisest man in the land, the king sent him home and bade him return in four days to answer four challenging questions to prove his wisdom.

When the bishop arrived home, he took off his mitre and sobbed, knowing that if he couldn't answer a single question he would surely lose his head. At that moment, a shepherd was passing by and listened to the bishop's story.

"Give me your clothes and your mitre and I will visit the king pretending to be you. If I can't answer the king's questions, he will only take the life of a lowly shepherd and not a man of God."

So the shepherd was on his way and the king was ready with some difficult questions.

"How fast can I travel around the world?" the king asked, peering at the shepherd.

"Why, your majesty, if you have a horse that can follow the sun, it will take you twenty-four hours."

The king blinked at the shepherd's cleverness, but couldn't deny his answer.

"Now how far is it from heaven to earth?" The king glared.

"Why your majesty, I am certain that you are an expert stone thrower, so it's only a stone's throw."

Taken aback by the shepherd's flattery, the king launched one more question.

"Can you tell me how much I am worth?"

"You are only worth twenty-eight pieces of silver. Jesus was sold for thirty pieces and I would think he was worth at least two more pieces than your majesty."

Blustering, the king shouted, "Can you tell me what I am thinking?"

"You think that I am a clever bishop, but I'm nothing but a shepherd."

The king then spared the bishop and made the shepherd his chancellor.

■ ■ ■

Cleverness is always rewarded, but in investing, it's honesty, modest expenses, and performance that really count, so don't be hoodwinked by appearances and claims.

CHAPTER 11

Putting It All Together: Portfolios for Any Market

There are many good reasons why an investor might decide to sell common stocks. He may want to build a new home or finance his son in a business. Any one of a number of similar reasons can, from the standpoint of happy living, make selling common stocks sensible.

—Philip Fisher

In the ever-expanding sphere of the ego, the space around the self is boundless. It knows no limits since the universe itself is infinite and mortality is keeping pace with medical technology. It is clearly a time of energy, sound, and furious activity in the global economy. We all want to be part of it. Some of us shared in the wealth by taking our home equity to build a larger home; others invested in the stock market. We felt wealthier because of heftier 401(k) balances, six-figure home-equity stakes, the cars in the driveway, and the vacations to the Caribbean. Ego space, however, is abstract, a derivative of expectation and speculation. We build the big homes because we think we'll be able to afford the mortgage, taxes, and upkeep over time. And we don't even consider the thought of downsizing, except maybe when the kids are out of the house or it's time to live near a golf course in Florida. Like outer space, ego space is filled with all sorts of perils. There's lots of radiation from the glare of the small screen, screaming at us to buy or sell without rhyme or reason. If we don't have the right insulation around us, we're fried. There are meteors and asteroids and the sheer vacuum of space itself, so we have to bring our own oxygen. Only when we prepare for the perils can we truly mitigate the risks.

Speaking of risk, having written five books on investing and countless magazine articles, I have to confess that I have made many investing mistakes. I invested in sector funds and moved out at the wrong time. I panicked and pulled out of stocks during the October 1987 crash and missed some of the rebound. I invested in gold-mining shares after there was a spurt in inflation. When inflation went away, I pulled out too late. I invested in foreign emerging-markets funds after their best year, then stayed in too long during their dog years. I invested in a portfolio of solid blue-chips with DRIPs, only to pull out when prices were down and I could've reaped some incredible gains if I just held on for a few years. And worst of all, I concentrated too much money in technology and telecommunications, ignoring vast pieces of the market. So I have dwelled in ego space and it is not a prosperous place.

The most obvious problem with my family portfolio was that (1) I neglected watching it carefully year to year (moving twice and having a baby won't help your attention span), (2) I failed to state our long-term objectives and stick to them, and (3) it just wasn't diversified. It took me several months of research to figure out the next move. Here's what we did (and you can do this with your own portfolio in principle):

Prune the losers. I had one stock that we had held on to for five years. I bought at $2.50 and it languished at $1.50. It was a technology company that was producing MRI machines, but the company never posted a profit. It looked good on paper. However, management wasn't interested in boosting shareholder value, so I sold it at a loss. We also looked at our stock mutual funds, which were down more than 20 percent. We decided that this was more than we were prepared to lose, so we exchanged those shares for shares in other stock funds (read on).

Eliminate concentrated risk and duplications. Both my wife and I had several technology or health-care sector funds. That concentrated the risk in two industries, which are both extremely volatile. The technology funds got hit the worst, so they were sold and shares were exchanged for other, more diversified funds. Again, the volatility was too much for us. It was like we were parking our aircraft carriers in Pearl Harbor. At the time, we thought that putting more assets into two booming sectors would increase our profits, when in reality it gave us greater exposure to losses when the market turned. I also had a SEP-IRA in a zero-coupon bond fund, which focused risk on *one* type of bond that only profits from capital appreciation (and no interest) when long-term interest rates fall (they didn't). So, after two years of flat performance, I moved those shares into another fund. The biggest mistake I made was not considering my wife's holdings and mine as *one* portfolio, so it was constructed willy-nilly without regard to style, capitalization, or risk concentration. Now all of our 401(k) rollover IRA, SEP-IRAs, Roth IRAs, and Education IRAs for our two daughters are looked at as a whole portfolio. We also consolidated nearly all of the accounts with a low-cost mutual fund company that allowed us to monitor the portfolio on-line. All of the funds carried some of the lowest expense ratios in the business and no sales charges.

OUR NEW ALLOCATIONS

Style/Capitalization	Percentage Allocated (approximately)
Mid-/small-cap value stocks	30%
Large-cap value stocks	20%
Large-/mid-cap growth	20%
Small-cap growth index	10%
Equity-income (blend) funds	5%
Health/financial sector funds	5%
Global stock fund	5%
REIT index fund	5%

What styles and capitalizations did we ignore? After a careful look at our portfolio, I was surprised that nearly all of it was in large-cap growth stocks. So I took the money from the funds we sold out of and invested in the new ones on page 171.

Restructure the income portfolio. This took even more time and consideration than the stock portion of our portfolio. Before our reallocation, we kept 100 percent of our short-term cash in a tax-free money-market account and checking account. We only kept enough money in the checking account to pay monthly bills; the surplus went right to the money-market account for funds we would need within two years or less. Having learned the lesson from concentrating too much risk in similar stock funds, I decided to create another tier for our income needs: money we wouldn't need for more than a year and less than five years. In this part of our income portfolio, we agreed to take a little more risk, but quantified that risk to be a potential loss of no more than 5 percent of principal in exchange for a greater return. So we took 25 percent of the money sitting in our money-market fund and put 65 percent of it into a short-term bond index fund and 25 percent into a total bond-market index fund investing in a variety of corporate and government bonds. These funds yielded between 5 percent and 6.25 percent. That way, we mixed low and moderate-risk bonds within a small portion of our income portfolio. Why did we take 25 percent of the money out of the money market? We figured what a year's worth of expenses would be and invested the extra money at greater risk because we wouldn't be using the money for more than a year.

Since we anticipated—and planned for—a drop in our federal tax bracket, the tax-free money-market fund no longer made sense as it was barely yielding 2 percent in tax-equivalent dollars (the yield subtracted by the marginal tax rate). After subtracting the expenses for managing this fund, we were losing money after inflation. So I searched the Internet for the highest-yielding, lowest-cost money-market fund available (see www.imoneynet.com) and moved most of our short-term money into a new account yielding about 3.25 percent, boosting our returns by more than 50 percent. I even found a large, reputable money-fund manager that was waiving all management expenses (a fairly common practice in the business) until 2006, so that also boosted return.

In addition to the income portfolio restructuring, we also refinanced our mortgage. After months of negotiation and delays, we were able to negotiate a no-escrow mortgage at a rate a full percentage point below our previous mortgage. That saved us $100 a month and allowed us to invest the money we needed for taxes in an interest-bearing vehicle such as a U.S. Treasury note, which would not only guarantee the principal, but pays us interest (as opposed to not earning a dime in the bank's escrow account). The refinancing alone saved us $1,200 a year.

The bear market, in retrospect, prompted us to think carefully about how to best allocate risk. In boom times, you tend to be floating in ego space, hallucinating about the dancing bubble bear, so none of these ideas occur to you. All of what we've done is hardly the perfect model for what *you* need to do, although we managed to balance risk within our portfolio and enhance returns in every way possible. Everyone is different. You need to start, as I mentioned in chapter 2, by gauging what your short-term needs are and making sure you have enough cash for emergencies and ongoing expenses for at least a year. This is your "safe" money, which you put into vehicles that preserve principal. Beyond that, you are investing for intermediate needs and ratchet up risk accordingly.

You will be able to outlast bear markets if you keep your short-term income safe and diversify your intermediate- and long-term investments across styles, capitalizations, sectors, and asset classes (stocks, bonds, real estate, cash). And keep in mind the risks in your own life. Is your job situation unsteady? Are you in an unstable industry? Are you self-employed? Find out how much you are spending on monthly items and see what can be cut back. Keep enough cash on hand to get you through the down cycles in your business. Also quantify your risk in every fund and stock so that it's spread out among high-, moderate-, and low-risk vehicles. Know

RISK AND RETURN FOR VARIOUS INVESTMENT STRATEGIES

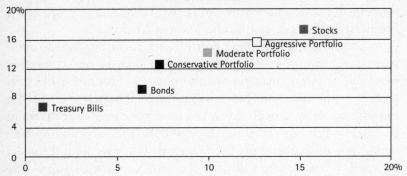

Average Annual Return

Risk (Annualized Standard Deviation, % per year)

The chart shows the risk/reward trade-off of 30-day U.S. Treasury bills (Lehman Brothers U.S. Aggregate Index), and stocks (Russell 3000) and for three portfolios composed of these asset classes, Conservative (40% stocks/40% bonds/20% Treasury bills), Moderate (60/30/10), and Aggressive (80/20/0). Figures are annualized for the 20-year period ended 12/31/99.

Lehman Brothers U.S. Aggregate Index—an unmanaged index comprised of U.S. goverment, investment-grade corporate, asset-backed, and mortgage-backed securities.
Russell 3000—an unmanaged index that measures the performance of the 3,000 largest companies based on total market capitalization, which represents approximately 98% of the investable U.S. market.
Source: T. Rowe Price Associates.

how much you can lose in each fund or stock by looking at their worst years in addition to the winning years. All of this information is available from your public library and will take you only a few minutes to digest.

After you do your homework, you can build a bear-proof portfolio and not worry about it. There are a number of misconceptions, however, that get in our way as we navigate ego space. The colliding asteroids of emotion and faulty logic are immense when it comes to the market, but they can be overcome. As we conclude our journey, I'd like to suggest some ways of dealing with emotional barriers and making changes.

Overcoming Barriers: Asking the Right Questions

Much of what is known about investment risk is clearly detailed in every mutual-fund prospectus, which, unfortunately, most people neglect to read. It's an important starting point for understanding what could go wrong and how to avoid trouble. If you are scouting an individual company, read the company's annual report, "10-k" SEC filing, and any independent analysts' reports from Value Line, S&P, Morningstar, and other firms.

- **Pay attention to objectives.** Every mutual fund must tell you what the fund is trying to do. Is the manager aiming for growth through capital appreciation or income or both? What kinds of stocks are they buying? If you need income, you have no business in a stock fund seeking capital appreciation. Know where you want to be and see if the fund's objective matches yours. You can also discuss this directly with a broker. Is the stock or bond appropriate for *your* objectives and risk tolerance?
- **What are the investment strategies?** What kinds of securities will the fund buy? How will they select the securities? Are they using a value or growth approach? What percentage of the securities will be allocated by sector or country? Feel free to call the fund company or manager to get your questions answered. They will talk to you.
- **Special investment risks.** Pay special attention to this section of the prospectus. What's the downside? What kinds of securities may go belly up in a storm? What percentage of the portfolio will be comprised of the riskiest assets? How much more volatility will special risks add to the returns of the portfolio?
- **Who should invest?** This language is usually fairly clear. Is the fund or security low, moderate, or high risk? What does that mean

for this fund? In terms of a bond fund, you can ask what will happen to the value of this fund if interest rates rise 1 percent. Or with stocks, what happens to this fund if there's a downturn? How does the fund compare to the index? Explain why you are investing and what you are seeking. How long do you have to invest? Short-term goals are best served through funds that preserve capital; long-term goals are best served through higher risk and capital appreciation.

▪ **What are the expenses of the fund?** Ask for the expense ratio of the fund. Compare it to average expenses for similar funds. What are the commissions, back-end loads, marketing charges (12b-1 fees), and other expenses. What are those costs over time? They make a big difference if you don't plan to sell for a long time.

▪ **How can you get your money out?** With mutual funds, you can arrange wire transfers to your savings or checking accounts, write a check, or request a redemption. With DRIPs, it gets a little tricky because you have to go through a transfer agent and it may take several weeks. If you ask these questions, you have a greater likelihood of matching the fund or security to your investment goals.

What Misconceptions May Interfere With Your Investment Success?

It's also helpful to know what kinds of thought processes may interfere with your asking the right questions and making the right decisions. The field of economics called "behavioral finance" seeks to explain investor psychology. Led by the University of Chicago's Richard Thaler, this subspecialty has found a number of consistently dangerous behavior patterns in the ego space of investors.

Investors often employ flawed logic in making decisions, which hastens the loss of their money. Here are a few trouble spots to watch out for:

Holding on too long. We tend to hoard losers and sell off winners. The value school of investing, for example, takes the opposite tack. You need to keep your winners and shed your losers. Most people hope to recoup their losses and buy more shares of a loser rather than sell it and buy a stock that's growing. If you have a loser—a stock that's down more than 20 percent—sell it. Uncle Sam will let you write off some of the losses.

Buying high, selling low. As I mentioned in chapter 9, this is a perennial fault of investors largely based on the "bigger jackpot effect." When investors see a stock move skyward, they assume that it will continue forever, no matter how overvalued that stock may be. Just because other investors assign a high p/e or high stock price doesn't mean it's worth buying. And once they buy the high-priced stock, they stay put for a while until the inevitable decline, sell, and lock in the loss, or they hold on, thinking they will get back to the price at which they bought the stock. If you have the gumption—and all of the fundamentals of a stock look good—stay the course. How long will you wait? If nothing happens in a year, will you sell? Take a look at your portfolio once a year. If you have losers, prune them.

Believing stock analysts. "Hot" research analysts—the talking heads you see on TV who work for brokerage houses—are there for a reason. They are there to sell you on stocks, not to share with you any profitable insights. They are pitchmeisters who are there to manipulate you into buying so that the price of their recommended stocks goes up. And it's no coincidence that the stocks they are pitching are the same stocks sold by their brokerage house. It's amazing that this persistent and undeniable conflict of interest hasn't gotten more people in trouble. All too many people suspend reality when they look at the small screen, the ultimate window to investor ego space.

Knowing the "right" time to invest. There are always investors who claim to know when the market will "turn." So they plunge in and out at the wrong times. Not even Alan Greenspan knows what's going on with the stock market. Either stay fully invested in your portfolio or stay away from it entirely if you have a short-term focus.

Getting the best advice. I'm constantly amazed at how many extremely educated people are willing to take advice from a complete stranger on what stock or mutual fund to buy. Investing is a very personal matter. You have to know yourself before you invest. Nobody else can plot the right course for you, your family, or the amount of risk that will allow you to rest easily.

Overtrading costs too much. Let's say you are completely enveloped in your investor ego and are convinced you know every time a stock is overpriced or headed for a fall, or the market is turning. Every time you act on your conviction, you will certainly pay a commission to your broker and taxes on your profit (if you have them). Had you just done quality research and held on to the stocks for twenty years, you would have done much better. *Morningstar Stock Investor* found that, after taxes, $10,000 invested in a "buy and hold" stock portfolio netted you $77,170, but only $52,546 if you sold each stock after one year. You can become overconfident and trade too much simply because you trust the (often bad) advice of others. "Overconfidence-based trading is truly hazardous to accumulating wealth!" warns John Nofsinger in *Investment Madness: How Psychology Affects Your Investing . . . and What to Do about It* (Prentice Hall, 2001).

All of these factors add to the risks that you can easily avoid. If you don't want to guess where the market is going, buy a mix of index funds and hold them. Only sell them if you need the money. If you want to add some spice to your portfolio, choose from any of the managed funds I've recommended in this book. While it sounds counterintuitive, buying and holding stocks and funds is one of the simplest, no-brainer ways to wealth because your risk goes down over time. Perhaps one of the best writers on the subject of risk is Peter Bernstein, who wrote the classic *Against the Gods: The Remarkable Story of Risk* (Wiley, 1996). Bernstein, a money manager, profiled the history of risk, risk management, and insurance in his noteworthy book. One passage stood out that summed up the field of behavioral finance:

> A growing volume of research reveals that people yield to inconsistencies, myopia, and other forms of distortion throughout the process of decision-making. That may not

matter much when the issue is whether one hits the jack-pot or the slot machine or picks a lottery number that makes dreams come true. But the evidence indicates that these flaws are even more apparent in areas where the con-sequences are more serious.

DON'T TIME THE MARKET: IT WILL COST YOU
$10,000 investment in the S&P 500,
3/1/96 through 3/3/01

Period of Investment

Over the 5-year period from March 1, 1996 through March 31, 2001, an investor who jumped out of the market during down periods would have seriously lowered his or her returns. Being out of the market, as measured by the S&P 500 Index, for just the 10 best days (out of 3,653 days) would have reduced returns by nearly 35%. Being out of the market for the best 40 days would have cost an investor nearly 70% of the potential returns over the period.

Source: Invesco.

Knowing When to Sell

If you want to participate in a triathlon, you know that you're going to be doing a lot of running, biking, and swimming to get in shape for the actual event. If your knees get sore or you pull a mus-cle, you have to stop training for a while. The discipline of invest-ing is much the same, only investors spend more time on their bodies than on making the right decisions with their money.

Bear markets prompt a lot of serious thinking about investment objectives, timing, and fine-tuning portfolios. I know it did for my wife and me and all of my family and friends. The plunge in the market forced us to make some changes that we wouldn't have considered in a booming market, changes that we should have been thinking about all along. Knowing when to sell is more important in many ways than knowing when and how to buy. Americans can buy anything. It's as easy as eating ice cream. Selling, however, is not something we are good at. It's like getting rid of a favorite possession. We want to hold on no matter what. Here are some guidelines for stocks and mutual funds that will prove useful in any market, so that you don't have to hold on to losers:

▪ **Set your loss limits.** Brokers call this "stop-loss." You set a price at which you will sell. For mutual funds, you have to look at percentage losses. How much of a loss will you tolerate? Know the answer before going in. Look at the fund's performance during its worst year. Would you stay invested if you were in the fund during an off year? Maybe the fund is too volatile to begin with, and you have no business being in it. Research before you invest.

▪ **What has changed?** Sometimes companies hit a rough patch in the economy or their sector. When oil prices go up, airlines and trucking companies get clobbered because their cost of doing business goes up. When commodity prices rise, a number of companies get hit hard. Is there something fundamentally wrong with management? Motorola, for example, bet on the wrong standard for cell phones and they lost tremendous market share. If something can be fixed, is management fixing it? Most corporations' standard response to trouble in their business is to cut costs and lay off people, but they may be missing the core problems. You have to be tough in asking the questions about whether a company or fund's woes are short-term or long-term.

▪ **Bad news travels fast.** If one company reports lower earnings in a line of business, chances are others will, too. Unless a company is broadly diversified, one suffering sector can pull them down. Ideally, you want a company or fund participating in a growing business, but that's hard to find in a slack economy, so you may need to sell if there's no hope on the horizon.

▪ **Have a sell target.** If you have a target for short-term appreciation, and you don't intend to invest in the stock or fund short term, then set a sell target and stick to it. If the stock doesn't hit the target by a certain time, sell it.

▪ **Are fundamentals getting worse?** Is net income on a downward trend? Are sales decreasing? Are earnings per share dropping? Is the company losing market share? Are operating margins falling? These are all signs that you should be selling.

▪ **What are the insiders doing?** By insiders, I mean executives of the company. Are they fleeing the ship by selling huge amounts of shares? Each company is required to report that information to the Securities and Exchange Commission. It's also listed in the *Wall Street Journal,* in *Barron's,* and throughout the Internet. Don't buy or sell based on "inside" information; it's usually somebody touting a stock with an undue sense of self-importance.

▪ **What is inflation doing?** Double-digit inflation ravages the bond and stock markets in different ways. With bonds, inflation pushes up interest rates and depresses bond prices. For companies, they must shell out more for materials, operating expenses, and labor and can't always recoup those expenses by charging more to their customers. So stock prices get hurt as well, although small stocks fare somewhat better than bonds in an inflationary economy. As John Neff notes, "Inflation becomes a bogeyman that can distort all of your painstaking, bottom-up calculations. Double-digit inflation devastates fixed-income markets and, in consequence, ravages equity markets. A whole new standard emerges." If inflation rears its ugly head, the last place you want to be is in a long-term bond fund. In an inflationary recession, this can be disastrous.

▪ **Did the company's product become a commodity?** If you had invested in a mutual fund dominated by cell phone makers or computer resellers, you know what happened. Every cycle of new technology makes yesterday's products obsolete. Make sure you are investing in innovators on the manufacturing and marketing side or find fund managers who are good at finding leading-edge companies.

- **Don't fall in love.** With a stock, that is. Capitalism makes fools of us all. Markets change, technology changes. Not every company or fund can keep up with the new product cycles. You don't know more than the market does.

- **Did your mother ask about the stock?** I always know the Chicago Cubs are headed for a fall when my mother mentions them. Of course, the Cubs always fall and she only mentions them because she's sick of my dad complaining about them, which he's been doing for the last fifty years. Unless your mother is an investor, you don't want to see your stock's CEO on the cover of *Time, Newsweek,* or *U.S. News & World Report.* That's a death knell. Stocks and mutual funds can get too popular. With mutual funds, the main problem is trying to invest all the money pouring in after a winning year. They can't get it invested fast enough, so they either close the fund or make mistakes.

- **Sell to take profits.** If the market's up 20 percent, take some profits and put them in cash or another stock that's underpriced. Don't pay any attention to the general market, however. Pay attention to the companies and funds you own.

- **If dividends aren't there, time to dump.** If you bought a fund or stock because it paid dividends, it should be raising its dividend payout consistently every year. There are plenty of companies with excellent dividend payout rates, so you don't have to stay with a loser.

- **Never sell for tax reasons.** You may be avoiding the real reason why you need to sell some shares: they're losing money. Keep in mind that the more you trade, the higher your transaction costs (and taxes, if you are selling winners), and the lower your total return.

- **You're not going to break even.** This is one of the greatest deceptions in holding losers: the idea that if we hold a fund or stock long enough, it will get back to where we bought it. If you're waiting for that to happen in a mutual fund, fund management is charging for expenses and transactions, so you just get deeper in the hole. With stocks, it's better to take the loss and put the money into cash than hold onto a position that's earning nothing.

- **Forget about short-term results.** Richard Thaler found that we tend to give more weight to recent performance than historical returns. As I cited in the last chapter, when tech stocks were at their peak in 2000, more than half of the new money in tech funds was coming in. I would bet that most of those investors didn't bother to check to see how volatile those funds were over time. The opposite kind of investor doesn't take enough risk because of "loss aversion," the chance that they'll lose a dollar or two in today's market, so they ignore the fact that stocks are the best performing class of financial assets over decades—and their chances of making money are 80 percent or better.

- **Don't watch the price every day.** If you are watching the tube every day, it will drive you nuts. Evaluate your portfolio once a year. As Philip Carret advises in *The Art of Speculation* (Wiley, 1997), "It is conventional advice to the investor that he should go over his holdings in search of weak spots at least annually."

What We Know about Investing: A Review

We need to do a little review of the field trips we've taken. Here's what we've covered so far:

1. Stocks beat bonds over time, but not all the time. Long-term stock returns may be lower, so we need to prepare for that possibility by diversifying our stock holdings and keeping enough cash for our needs.

2. Cash and bonds are essential for short-term income needs—and an occasional buffer from the stock market—but won't beat inflation over time (stocks will). Even a little real estate helps in tempering risk in the portfolio.

3. Mixing bonds and stocks will reduce overall risk, particularly in down markets. A sensible mixture of 60 percent stocks to 40 percent bonds, in a "balanced" mix or mutual fund, will help get us through bear markets.

4. Fine-tuning the combination of stocks and bonds will mean looking for both kinds of vehicles in a "value" perspective, where securities are bought at bargain prices and held for the long term.

5. Over the long term, the value perspective does the best in identifying stocks and bonds that will perform well in any market. We can either do the research ourselves or hire top fund managers.

6. Investing in smaller-cap and mid-cap stocks over time will further enhance returns with considerably lower risk over time in a broadly diversified portfolio.

7. Stocks and bonds from overseas will also lower the risk profile of our portfolios because foreign markets may move in different directions than domestic markets.

8. We can build a diversified portfolio ourselves through dividend reinvestment plans (DRIPs) and do the research ourselves on a portfolio of individual stocks.

9. If we want to boost returns, we can invest in specific sectors of the stock market, but only if we are committed to investing in these vehicles for at least ten years and make these funds part of a diversified approach.

10. By understanding how excessive costs chew up returns over time, prudent investments in index funds can reduce expenses, lower risk, and give us broad exposure to every kind of stock, bond, and real estate market.

Okay, that wasn't so bad, was it? It's easier than doing your taxes or worrying about Social Security. These principles are fairly universal and you can employ them as long as you like. They are based on the collective wisdom, insight, and research of some of the finest minds in investing. And they work over time. All you have to do is put the plan in motion and hold on through the down cycles. Unfortunately, most investors will not stay the course and continue to trade on tips from their brother-in-law, "someone who knows," and brokerage house analysts touting something their company already owns and is trying to hawk to the masses.

Investing is a discipline. In order to be successful, you start with a few guidelines, but need some insights into human nature before you can proceed. You know your needs fairly well, so you need to find a portfolio that creates harmony with the rest of your life, an ecology that is sustainable for the amount of risk you can take. So here are a few suggestions for how to do that:

In Search of the Right Allocation: My Portfolio Advice

When a fisherman prepares his line, he has a specific lure or bait he uses to catch a certain type of fish. Bullheads won't go after flies. Trout don't like plastic worms. Your portfolio needs to be properly baited to catch the right returns. Now it's a question of which funds to select and what percentage of which type will work for you (regarding individual stock allocations, refer to chapter 8 for some broad suggestions).

The conventional wisdom in investment research is that 90 percent of the variability in returns is due to *asset allocation*, that is, the portions of your portfolio invested in specific vehicles. For example, a 100 percent bond portfolio will produce returns that are far different from a 100 percent stock portfolio. Since diversification is the best way to go for every kind of investor, I have some suggestions as to how you can produce returns that are acceptable given your level of risk tolerance.

With mutual funds, the question of consistent returns is always a nagging problem for investors. Some 40 percent of the variation in returns among similar funds is explained by asset allocation. Two similar funds may invest in large-company stocks, but one may turn over the portfolio faster, have a higher expense ratio, or lose a top manager. So you need to look for low-expense funds with performances that beat their peers over time. At least five years' worth of performance information is a good starting point; ten years or more is better.

The following portfolios are structured for investors at different points in their lives with varying tolerances for risk. You can tailor the percentages any way you like. You can use the funds I've suggested in this book in the "fund type" slots—if the funds' risk profiles truly match your risk tolerance and objectives. You can mix and match funds to construct the portfolio that's best for you.

NERVOUS NELLIE SAVER PORTFOLIO

Profile: You don't like volatility, but need income short-term, capital preservation, and some growth.

Fund Type	Allocation
Money-market fund	40%
Short-term bond fund	10%
Intermediate-term bond fund	10%
Equity-income/balanced fund	20%
Large-cap value fund	20%

EMPTY NESTERS

The kids are out of the house, college bills are paid, everyone's in good health, and you need to save for retirement in 10 to 15 years. Growth is needed, but capital preservation is also important.

Fund Type	Allocation
Money-market fund	10%
Intermediate-term bond fund	10%
Equity-income or balanced fund	20%
Small- or mid-cap value fund	20%
Large-cap value fund	20%
Large-cap growth or sector fund	10%
International stock fund	10%

LET IT RIDE!

Retirement is at least 20 years away and growth is paramount, so above-average risk is tolerable. Short-term expenses can be covered in a money-market fund.

Fund Type	Allocation
Small-cap value	30%
Small- or mid-cap growth	20%

Large-cap growth/value	20%
Sector	10%
International	10%
Real estate	10%

GOAL-ORIENTED: SHORT-TERM SAVINGS

You are saving for a downpayment on something big within five years (home, college, etc.). Market risk needs to be at the absolute minimum and capital preservation is paramount.

Fund Type	Allocation
Money market	60%
Short-term bond	20%
Intermediate-term bond	10%
Government agency bonds (short)	10%

FDIC-insured CDs or Treasury notes may be substituted for short- or intermediate-term bonds if capital preservation is paramount.

MIDDLE OF THE ROAD

Somewhat between "Let It Ride!" and "Nervous Nellie," this portfolio seeks long-term growth with at least a 15-year horizon. This is for investors who want low- to moderate-risk capital appreciation and no income (outside of short-term savings) for now.

Fund Type	Allocation
Equity-income/balanced fund	20%
Small- or mid-cap value	20%
Large-cap value	20%
Large-cap growth	20%
International	10%
Real estate	10%

SIMPLICITY INDEX

For long-term investors with at least a 15-year time horizon, this allocation won't need to change unless your needs change. Risk is average across the board. Investors whose needs reflect the profiles of the other portfolios can use index funds depending on their objective.

Fund Type	Allocation
Total market	50%
Small-cap value	20%
International	10%
Total bond market	10%
Real estate	10%

Not Another Fable

This story is about a young couple who bought a house in the country and two horses, and they were doing really well with a six-figure household income. The house was a hovel, but they fixed it up. The horses ran away now and again and the home remodeling got to be exorbitant, but our couple was making decent money in their jobs (the wife had her own thriving software business) and the stock market boomed during the '80s and '90s, so they spent the money on the ramshackle house and the husband continued to commute up to four hours a day to and from their country cottage.

Then a bright, blue-eyed baby girl named Sarah Virginia came along and the earth moved. Suddenly she needed friends to play with and a decent school district, and the horses had to go because they were downright dangerous because when Sarah became a toddler she liked to run through the horses' legs, scaring the parents half to death.

So our couple sold their little home in the country, sold the horses, and built a new house with twenty-four hundred square feet and a basement in a promising community with plenty of educational choices, a trail system, beach, organic farm, and lots of little kids, particularly little girls. They were happy for about a year and a half, even welcoming another blue-eyed baby girl, Julia Theresa, into the world. Their property tax bill was more than twice what they were paying on the old house, which had no basement or garage, but they figured they could easily cover it with their income. They were willing to pay the premium for all of the amenities and the lovely neighbors.

Then the husband's company disintegrated because his boss had spent all of the company's money and then some on a Web site that didn't bring a penny in the door. First the Web site was shut down and lots of people lost their jobs. Then the husband lost *his* job and health insurance after fifteen years of steady employment in the middle of a recession. The stock market continued to have seizures and suddenly our couple didn't feel quite so wealthy anymore. Unfortunately, the wife had sidelined her business to spend time with her beautiful daughters, so she was worried, too.

Our family, fortunately, did okay, because they had been saving all along to avoid financial catastrophe, putting a year's worth of expenses into a money-market fund and moving their long-term savings into safer, less-aggressive mutual funds. They had also been investing all along in individual stocks through a family stock investment club and fully funded their SEP-IRAs, 401(k)s, Roth IRAs, and Education IRAs (read my *Kitchen-Table Investor* for more details). When the husband lost his job, they cut back their spending to the absolute minimum and refinanced the mortgage.

Now the family is at home together twenty-four hours a day, the daughters are being educated by full-time parents, who work side by side during the kids' nap time. And that's not the end of the story, for this was the family's preferred mode of living all along. We're going to pull through.

. . .

You can choose the life you want. It can be done. A Harvard study of 724 men over a sixty-year period found that the men lived to a ripe old age largely *by choice*. They generally chose the path of "moderate alcohol use, no smoking, regular exercise, appropriate weight and positive coping mechanisms."

Harmonious living is an integral part of a sound personal ecology—one that is balanced between work, family, community, and leisure. When it comes to investing, you need moderation as well to get you through the growling times of crisis, doubt, depression, and indecision. It all starts with a sober attitude toward risk, a close focus on your investment goals, and a diligent savings plan. The rest is a saga of your own making, lovingly crafted to your life in ways that are important to you.

References

Chapter 1. Dancing Bubble Bears: A Brief History of Bear Markets, Booms, Busts, Risks, and What to Expect

Bacon, Francis, *The Essays of Francis Bacon* (Peter Pauper Press). Reading Sir Francis, I am utterly convinced he was *not* Shakespeare, although he did have some worthwhile things to say on a number of subjects.

Berman, Dennis, "Former Lucent CEO Was Granted Severance Package of $12.5 Million," *The Wall Street Journal*, 14 August 2001. Even losers are winners. What a great country.

Hay, Peter, ed., *The Book of Business Anecdotes* (Facts on File, 1988), pp. 61–62. A fine collection of vignettes.

Browning, E. S., "Normal Stock Return Lies in the Eye of Beholder," *The Wall Street Journal*, 27 April 2001.

"Corporate Durability: A Talent for Longevity," *The Economist*, 14 April 2001. A short piece on companies that have survived nearly a century.

Clements, Jonathan, "Investors Should Prepare for Pain, Too," *The Wall Street Journal*, 9 June 2001. A pointed piece by one of the best investment columnists writing today.

Ibbotson Associates, *Stocks, Bonds, Bills, and Inflation: 2001 Yearbook*. This compendium of historical returns for stocks and bonds is quoted throughout the book.

Shiller, Robert, *Irrational Exuberance* (Broadway, 2000), p. 195. A sober, if not overly pessimistic, view of stock market returns.

Bogle, John, "The Implications of Style Analysis for Mutual Fund Performance Evaluation," *Journal of Portfolio Management*, Summer 1998. A long-winded title for a landmark paper on mutual fund style, risk management, and returns.

Clements, Jonathan, "Vanguard's Brennan Offers a Refresher Course," *The Wall Street Journal*, 29 May 2001. It all comes down to diversification.

Siegel, Jeremy, *Stocks for the Long Run: The Definitive Guide to Financial Markets, Returns and Long-Term Investment Strategies* (McGraw-Hill, 1998). Definitive and pragmatic, read this after *Irrational Exuberance*.

Bernstein, Richard, *Navigate the Noise: Investing in the New Age of Media and Hype* (Wiley, 2001), p. 149. If you need some insight as to how to ignore all market hype, this is an indispensable volume.

Chapter 2. Cash Is King, or Is It? Short-Term Ways of Reducing Risk and Finding Balance

Rukeyser, Merryle, *The Common Sense of Money and Investments* (Wiley, 1988), p. 306. A no-frills classic on investing by Lou Rukeyser's dad.

Morningstar Mutual Funds Conference, Chicago, June 26, 2001. Bill Gross was a keynoter at the conference, from which his profile is excerpted. Also see Morningstar Mutual Funds' reports on the many bond funds Gross manages. Eric Jacobson authored the reports, which are posted on www.morningstar.com.

Ibbotson Associates, *Stocks, Bonds, Bills, and Inflation: 2001 Yearbook*.

"401(k) Time Frames," *Mutual Funds*, February 2001. A fairly decent roundup of what happened to mutual funds in 2000.

Simon, Ruth, "Bank on It: Savings Accounts Find New Fashion," *The Wall Street Journal*, 15 August 2001. With the stock market swooning, investors look to bank savings vehicles as safe harbors.

Graham, Benjamin, *The Intelligent Investor* (Harper & Row, 1973), p. 13. Still required reading for any serious stock investor.

Rothchild, John, *The Bear Book: Survive and Profit in Ferocious Markets* (Wiley, 1998), p. 150. Offers ample detail on down markets and sound strategies.

Buchan, James, *Frozen Desire: The Meaning of Money* (Farrar, Straus & Giroux, 1997). A thoroughly elegant and informed history of money. A must-read.

"Are Bonds Suddenly *Tres* Sexy," *U.S. News & World Report*, 17 April 2000. When the market dropped, investors immediately fled to bonds.

Chapter 3. A Balanced Approach to Risk: Stocks, Bonds, and Real Estate in Perspective

Leopold, Aldo, "A Biotic View of Land," essay from 1939. I can read Aldo Leopold until kingdom come. His ecological point of view is timeless.

"Performance Update," *T. Rowe Price Report*, Summer 2001. A fine newsletter loaded with relevant investor facts. Check out their Web site at www.troweprice.com.

Background on PAX Balanced Fund on www.paxfunds.com. Although dedicated to the small PAX family of funds, there's some excellent background information on socially responsible investing. Also see the resource section Web sites, which follow this section.

Banta, Patrick, "When to Bring Your Stock Portfolio Home," *The Wall Street Journal*, 25 July 2001.

Banta, Patrick, "Existing Home Prices Accelerate Ascent," *The Wall Street Journal*, 14 August, 2001. Residential real estate is a fickle market as well.

Francis, David, "Once Fixer-Uppers, Real Estate Funds Shine," *The Christian Science Monitor*, 17 July, 2000. Real estate funds perked up when the stock market lost its luster.

Study from the National Association of Real Estate Investment Trusts, Chicago, Ill., 2001. Coolidge anecdote from *The Book of Business Anecdotes*.

Hagstrom, Robert, *The Essential Buffett: Timeless Principles for the New Economy* (Wiley, 2001), p. 65. Hagstrom is to Buffett what Boswell was to Johnson, although I am quoting Hagstrom on how Phil Fisher influenced the value school.

Chapter 4. Bargains and Income: Stocks and Bonds That Stand Up during the Storm

Graham, Benjamin, *The Intelligent Investor* (Harper & Row, 1973). Ben Graham is quoted widely in a number of books, although his is a nontechnical approach to the subject.

The Oakmark funds prospectus contained much of the background on their Equity-Income fund. Also consider their fine Select fund, which also has an excellent record. Other information was culled from an interview with Clyde McGregor at Oakmark's Chicago headquarters, 27 June 2001.

Andersen, Hans Christian, "The Princess and the Pea," from a collection of fairy tales by Hans Christian Andersen, ed. Margherita Osborne (Hampton Publishing, 1913). This charming collection never ages.

Liesman, Steve, "NASDAQ Companies' Losses Erase 5 Years of Profits," *The Wall Street Journal*, 16 August 2001. What is gained is lost in such a short period of time.

What Has Worked in Investing: Studies of Investment Approaches and Characteristics Associated with Exceptional Returns (Tweedy Browne, Inc., 2001). A sales piece dressed up as an academic paper, this collection of facts is loaded with topflight research studies on small-cap and value investing.

Hagstrom, Robert, *The Warren Buffett Way: Investment Strategies of the World's Greatest Investors* (Wiley, 1994), p. 39. Hagstrom's original view of Buffett and the value school offers some fresh insights.

Brandes, Charles, *Value Investing Today* (McGraw-Hill, 1998), p. 45. Although a little dated, a good introduction to the subject without the Buffettology.

Bernstein, Peter, *Against the Gods: The Remarkable Story of Risk* (Wiley, 1996). An ambitious, compelling account of risk management through the ages.

Cottle, Sidney, Roger Murray, and Frank Block, eds., *Graham & Dodd's Security Analysis*, 5th ed. (McGraw-Hill, 1988), p. 5. The mother lode for any fundamental or value investor, this text was originally published in the 1930s by Ben Graham. Definitely for serious investors only.

Chapter 5. Growth plus Value: How to Outsmart the Market

Loeb, Gerald, *The Battle for Investment Survival* (Wiley, 1996). Although dated in parts, still a good read.

Ibbotson Associates, *Stocks, Bonds, Bills, and Inflation: 2001 Yearbook*.

Bajkowski, John, "Performance Review 2000: Which Strategies Did Best?" *AAII Journal*, January 2001, p. 11. A fine overview of various stock-screening methods and how they did during 2001.

"Screening for Stocks Using a Dividend-Adjusted PEG Ratio," *AAII Journal*, www.aaii.com, August 2000. If you want to learn how to invest like retired fund manager John Neff, this is a good place to start.

Vick, Timothy, "Picking Stocks the Buffett Way: Understanding Return on Equity," *AAII Journal*, April 2001, p. 5. Some useful insights on understanding Warren Buffett's stockpicking style.

Belsky, Gary and Thomas Gilovich, *Why Smart People Make Big Mistakes— and How to Correct Them* (Simon & Schuster, 1999), p. 191. An enjoyable primer on investment psychology.

Plato, *The Republic*, Jowett translation (Modern Library). Socrates still speaks to us.

Chapter 6. Finding the Middle Ground: Mid-Cap and Small-Cap Investing

Walton, Izaak, *The Compleat Angler* (The Heritage Press, 1949). Although nominally about fishing, this treatise on life is perfect for that desert island (sans the *Survivor* crew).

John Rogers was interviewed in the Ariel world headquarters in Chicago, Ill. Other information on Ariel was gleaned from the fund prospectus and Ariel analysts.

Ibbotson Associates, *Stocks, Bonds, Bills, and Inflation: 2001 Yearbook*.

Burns, Scott, "Value, Fixed Income Leading 401(k) Derby," *The Daily Herald*, 7 August 2001. A snapshot of what did well during the 2001 debacle.

Vota, Scott, "Understanding Small-, Mid- and Large-Cap Stocks," *Trusts & Estates*, February 1999, p. 47. A gem of a piece that explains how these assets perform over time.

Friedman, Josh, "Microcaps Reaping Gains," *The Chicago Tribune*, 5 August 2001. The first shall be last and the last first.

Vernon-Jones, V. S., trans., *Aesop's Fables* (Avenal, 1912). Although this tale is estimated to be about twenty-five hundred years old, it still rings true.

Chapter 7. Values Abroad: And You Thought the Best Investments Were in the United States?

Maggio, Rosalie, comp., *Money Talks: Quotations on Money and Investing* (Prentice-Hall, 1998). A wonderful and witty compilation of money quotes.

T. Rowe Price Guide to International Investing (Baltimore, Md.: T. Rowe Price Associates), www.troweprice.com. A compilation of key research on international investing. T. Rowe Price has a number of useful educational articles and software packages for any investor.

Statman, Meir, "The Real Role of Foreign Stocks in an Investor's Portfolio," *AAII Journal*, June 2000. A suggested allocation of foreign stocks.

Morris, Charles, *Money, Greed and Risk: Why Financial Crises and Crashes Occur* (Century Foundation, 1994), p. 3. A great read if you need some perspective.

Chapter 8. Doing It Yourself: An Integrated Approach to Stocks

Maggio, Rosalie, comp., *Money Talks: Quotations on Money and Investing* (Prentice-Hall, 1998).

Power Investing with DRIPs newsletters, George Fisher, publisher. Much of the section on DRIPs is compiled from interviews with Fisher in mid-2001 and his newsletters (see resources section that follows).

Clements, Jonathan, "Dividends, Not Growth Is Wave of Future," *The Wall Street Journal*, 2 August 2001. Once again, Jon is on top of the trend toward more conservative investing.

Clements, Jonathan, "Time to Give Stocks the Green Light," *The Wall Street Journal*, 28 April 2001.

Saler, Thomas, *Taming the Bear: How to Invest in Stocks without Getting Eaten Alive* (Globe-Pequot, 1994), p. 49. Solid advice on down-market investing.

Franklin, Benjamin, *Poor Richard, An Almanack* (McKay, 1976). A constant companion that's even more durable than Ben's autobiography, which only goes to age thirty.

Chapter 9. Buying into Long-Term Trends and Holding On for Dear Life

Marcus Aurelius, *Meditations* (Mershon). The guy briefly portrayed by Richard Harris before he's murdered by his son in the movie *Gladiator*, he was a stoic philosopher given to some virtue when he wasn't persecuting Christians.

Morningstar Mutual Funds, www.morningstar.com, 28 April 2001. As with most of the mutual fund data quoted in the book, Morningstar is reliable, comprehensive, and useful in backgrounding funds.

Socially Responsible Fund Assets Report, published by PAX Funds, 8 August 2001. Although looking primarily at the growth in assets for socially responsible mutual funds, this report had some interesting insights into long-term societal trends. Available at www.paxfunds.com.

Weiss, Michael J., "The Demographic Investor," *American Demographics*, December 2000.

Clements, Jonathan, "Sector Funds Need a Warning Label," *The Wall Street Journal*, 14 August 2001. Jon nails sector fund investors who jump in at the last minute.

Vanguard Health Care Fund Prospectus, 17 August 2001. You never know what nuggets of information you'll find in a prospectus. I am an investor in this fund and have just moved my 401(k) and my wife's SEP-IRA accounts to Vanguard because they offer an array of funds at some of the lowest expense ratios in the business.

Davis, Robert, and David Wessel, *Prosperity: The Coming 20-Year Boom and What It Means to You* (Times, 1998), p. 11. While I don't agree with the basic premise, a solid work on the changing demographics and workforce.

"Mutual Fund Scorecard," *The Wall Street Journal*, 17 August 2001. This is their periodic overview of mutual-fund returns.

Grimm's Fairy Tales (Grossett & Dunlap). The Brothers Grimm collected some classics from throughout Europe; some of the tales are really weird and are designed to scare the wits out of kids.

Chapter 10. The Route to Simplicity: Index Funds Balance Costs and Boost Returns

Bogle John, "Selecting Equity Mutual Funds," *Journal of Portfolio Management*, Winter 1992. Not Bogle's best work, but certainly worth reading.

Kapoor, Kunal, *Morningstar Mutual Funds Quicktake Report*, www.morningstar.com, 31 May 2001. If you don't want the in-depth analysis of a full Morningstar report, you can find these thumbnail reports on their Web site.

TIAA-CREF Growth & Income Fund Prospectus, 1 April 2001. A sturdy competitor to Vanguard on the cost front, the huge pension-fund manager also publishes some readable and information prospecti that spell out risks quite clearly.

ICI Fact Book, 41st ed. (ICI, 2001). A little book chock-full of facts, published by the Investment Company Institute, the trade organization for the mutual fund industry. Also see their Web site at www.ici.org.

Bogle, John, *John Bogle on Investing: The First 50 Years* (McGraw-Hill, 2000). If you buy into Bogle's mantra that costs and indexing matter a lot to investors, you'll eat up this collection of speeches, papers, and his college dissertation from Princeton. Most of Bogle's wisdom, however, has been absorbed after seeing him speak over the last ten years at Morningstar mutual fund conferences. You can find a great deal of his insights at www.vanguard.com.

Lucchetti, Aaron, and Tom Lauricella, "Vanguard and S&P Seem Like Such a Nice Pair: Why the Nasty Spat?" *The Wall Street Journal*, 23 August 2001. The inside poop on Vanguard's dust-up with Standard & Poor's over the index Vanguard made famous.

ICI Fact Book, p. 40.

Kanon, Bloch Carré data from their Web site, www.kanon.com.

Bogle, *John Bogle on Investing*, p. 10.

Ibid., p. 27.

Bogle, John, "The Implications of Style Analysis for Mutual Fund Performance and Valuation," *Journal of Portfolio Management*, Summer 1998. I keep coming back to this in-your-face paper that was inspired by a Bogle speech. It's Bogle without apology.

In the Vanguard, Summer 2001. Not only did this fine newsletter feature the history of the index fund; it delved into long-term investment trends. See www.vanguard.com.

Petruno, Tom, "Money Managers Put to the Test," *Los Angeles Times*, 31 July 2001. Sometimes money managers can beat the index, but only for a while.

Rubino, John, *Main Street, Not Wall Street* (Morrow, 1998), p. 7. A useful introduction to investing in local/regional companies.

Thompson, Stith, ed., *One Hundred Favorite Folk Tales* (Indiana University Press, 1968). An engaging collection of tales from around the world. Nothing about Wall Street, however.

Chapter 11. Putting It All Together: Portfolios for Any Market

Fisher, Philip K., *Common Stocks and Uncommon Profits* (Wiley, 1975). If you can't figure out what's going on with Buffett's style—or don't want to do the math—the next best route is reading Phil Fisher, who is extremely accessible. This one's a hands-down classic.

Bernstein, Peter, *Against the Gods: The Remarkable Story of Risk* (Wiley, 1996), p. 265.

Neff, John, *John Neff on Investing* (Wiley, 1999). The legendary value investor reveals the core of his successful value style, which he employed at the Vanguard Windsor fund.

Cassidy, Donald, "When to Sell a Stock: Practical and Profitable Rules," *AAII Journal*, May 2001. Some really useful guidelines on when to dump a stock.

Glassman, James, "Long-Term Investors Are the Real Experts," *The Washington Post*, 31 March 1996. A dated, though relevant, piece on long-term investing.

Carret, Philip, *The Art of Speculation* (Wiley, 1997), p. 347. Although it was written looking back at the crash of 1929, there are still a few witty nuggets in this classic.

Nofsinger, John, *Investment Madness: How Psychology Affects Your Investing . . . and What You Can Do about It* (Prentice-Hall, 2001), p. 28. Another worthwhile read on investor psychology.

Ibbotson, Robert, and Paul Kaplan, "Does Asset Allocation Policy Explain 40%, 90% or 100% of Performance," *Financial Analyst's Journal*, January–February 2000.

Appendix 1: Resources

These are my favorite resources on investing, sampled from nearly every medium.

Books

Fisher, George C., *All About DRIPs and DSPs* (McGraw-Hill, 2001). Fisher covers the basics of DRIPs (dividend reinvestment plans) and DSPs (direct-purchase stock plans) with some suggested portfolios.

Staton, Bill, *America's Finest Companies Investment Plan* (Hyperion, 1998). A compendium on how to invest in blue-chip stocks.

Malkiel, Burton Gordon, *A Random Walk down Wall Street* (Norton, 2000). This paperback edition of the investment classic still makes so much sense, it's timeless.

Hoffman, Ellen, *Bankroll Your Future Retirement with Help from Uncle Sam* (Newmarket, 2001). Good information on retirement benefits.

Buffett, Mary, and David Clark, *Buffettology* (Fireside, 1999). Worthwhile companions to Robert G. Hagstrom Jr.'s books on Warren Buffett.

MacKay, Charles, *Extraordinary Delusions and the Madness of Crowds* (Crown, 1995). The undisputed 1841 classic on bubbles, manias, and market craziness.

Collins, Jim, *Good to Great: Why Some Companies Make the Leap . . . and Others Don't* (HarperBusiness, 2001). Provides some key insights on what makes for a solidly managed company over the long term.

Cottle, Sidney, Roger Murray, and Frank Block, eds., *Graham & Dodd's Security Analysis* (McGraw-Hill, 1988). Although no longer penned by Benjamin Graham and David Dodd, this is still the ultimate authority on security analysis, particularly for the Graham-Buffett value perspective. Actually, anything to do with security analysis is in this book, including the formulas you need to figure out return on equity and cash flow per share. This is not a page-turner, but you will find it invaluable if you are serious about investing on your own.

Carlson, Charles B., *Individual Investor Revolution: Seize Your New Powers of Investing and Make More Money in the Market* (McGraw-Hill, 2000). One-stop shopping for any novice stock investor, this generous volume has information on stockpicking, DRIPs, and general investment principles.

Fridson, Martin, *It Was a Very Good Year: Extraordinary Moments in Stock Market History* (Wiley, 2000). A collection of anecdotes on stock market highlights.

Ross, Nikki, *Lessons from the Legends of Wall Street: How Warren Buffett, Benjamin Graham, Phil Fisher, T. Rowe Price, and John Templeton Can Help You Grow Rich* (Dearborn, 2000). An engaging and concise read on the great investment minds of the last seventy-five years.

Delcourt, Paul, and Hazel Delcourt, *Living Well in the Age of Global Warming: 10 Strategies for Boomers, Bobos, and Cultural Creatives* (Chelsea Green, 2001). Which real estate and stocks do you buy down the road if global warming gets out of control? This offbeat book offers some answers.

Glickman, Marshall, *The Mindful Money Guide: Creating Harmony between Your Values and Your Finances* (Ballantine Wellspring, 1999). Although billed as a guide to socially responsible investing, this is a fine introduction to basic personal finance.

Walden, Gene, *The 100 Best Stocks to Own in America* (Dearborn, 2001). Updated every other year, this is a quick way to find some quality stocks.

Dreizler, Bob, *Tending Your Money Garden* (Rossonya, 2001). Although a personal finance book, this gentle title provides some perspective on socially responsible investing.

Clements, Jonathan, *25 Myths You've Got to Avoid—If You Want to Manage Your Money Right: The New Rules for Financial Success* (Simon & Schuster, 1999). I would call this the "best of Jon Clements." Invaluable all-around financial advice.

Miles, Robert P., *101 Reasons to Own the World's Greatest Investment: Warren Buffett's Berkshire Hathaway* (Wiley, 2001). While I wouldn't recommend this book's flag-waving for a single stock, the appendices are quite useful.

Columnists (Newspaper and Web Site)

Susan Bondy. Syndicated by the *Los Angeles Times* syndicate, Bondy is one of the newspaper industry's best generalists.

Scott Burns. A fine common-sense approach to investing and personal finance, Burns's Q&A's, syndicated from the *Dallas Morning News*, are often better than most columns.

Superstar Mutual Funds. Only available on www.cbs.marketwatch.com, Paul B. Farrell's no-nonsense message focuses on long-term investing.

Getting Going by Jonathan Clements. Dollar for dollar, Clements is not only the best columnist at the *Wall Street Journal,* he should be on your list of "must reads" every week.

Charles A. Jaffe on Mutual Funds. Based at the *Boston Globe* and syndicated across North America, Jaffe has the most current information on mutual funds.

Linda Stern. Syndicated by Reuters, Stern is often the voice of reason on most investment matters.

Databases

These resources are generally only found in the reference sections of libraries.

ABI/Inform. A prime source of background information on business and industry, featuring more than one thousand periodicals.

Business and Company Resource Center. A compendium of nearly two thousand business journals, fifteen hundred of them including full text.

Dun's Business Locator. Basic information on 10 million businesses located in the United States.

FIS Online. Fully searchable information on more than ten thousand publicly traded U.S. companies.

General BusinessFile ASAP (Infotrac). Some 960 periodicals are indexed, 460 of them with full text.

Organizations

The American Association of Individual Investors, www.aaii.com, (312) 280-0170, 625 North Michigan Avenue, Chicago, IL 60611. With more than 100,000 members and chapters in nearly every state, the AAII is a worthwhile educational stop if you do all of your own investing. Focused on securities analysis, the group supports all kinds of products and seminars tailored to individual investors. Membership is worth it just for access to their Web site, which is loaded with stock-screening software and archives of hundreds of articles on investing. Also worthwhile is their *AAII Journal*, which has current information on stocks, bonds, stock analysis techniques, insurance, mutual funds, and financial planning. They also publish annual guides to dividend reinvestment plans and no-load mutual funds.

Horizon Publishing, (800) 463-6596, 7412 Calumet Avenue, Hammond, IN 46324. Anchored by its flagship *Dow Theory Forecasts*, which has been published for the last fifty-seven years, Horizon has an array of newsletters and books for fundamental investors. Their *DRIP Investor* is the premier newsletter on DRIPs and stocks that have DRIPs.

Ibbotson and Associates, www.ibbotson.com, (312) 616-1620, 225 North Michigan Avenue, Suite 700, Chicago, IL 60601-7676. *The* wellspring of historical research on stocks and bonds, Ibbotson offers an array of products including its annual *Stocks, Bonds, Bills, and Inflation Yearbook*, which is a comprehensive record of the past performance of dozens of different investment classes. They also sell excellent presentation materials and investment analysis software.

Morningstar, www.morningstar.com, (800) 735-0700, 225 West Wacker Drive, Chicago, IL 60606. For years, Morningstar was the alpha and omega of mutual fund research, but recently emerged as a top stock-analysis firm, as well, with its *Stock Investor* newsletter. You can get Morningstar's top-drawer analyses on funds, stocks, and annuities on its Web site, on CD-ROM, or in printed form. They also produce a powerful software package called *Principia*, which crunches recent mutual-fund data to build the mutual-fund portfolio tailored to your risk/return profile. Also worthwhile for serious investors is their annual investment conference, which features the leading lights in mutual funds. If you are just scanning for a handful of mutual funds to round out your portfolio, though, check out their *Five-Star Investor* newsletter, which is available by subscription or in most libraries.

The National Association of Investors Corporation (NAIC), www.better-investing.org, (877) 275-6242, 711 West 13-Mile Road, Madison Heights, MI 48071. If you want to understand the fundamentals of stock and mutual-fund investing or are an investment club member (or want to join one or start one up), look no further. This nonprofit group of 550,000 members and 35,500 investment clubs is the mother ship of investment clubbing. They can tell you how to start up an investment club, how to keep it running, and how to pick stocks and mutual funds. Their excellent magazine *Better Investing* is not only highly readable, it's packed full of stories about investment clubs and their portfolios. They also sell software, have two DRIP plans, sponsor investment conferences, and have more than one hundred local chapters. Their publications are down-to-earth and useful whether you've just started to invest or have been investing on your own for years. Their "Top 100 Stocks" issue of *Better Investing* is a must read. They also have a program for young investors and a computer-assisted stock investment group.

Standard & Poor's, www.standardandpoors.com, (800) 221-7940, 25 Broadway, New York, NY 10004. The keeper of the S&P 500 Index also publishes some first-rate newsletters and reports for stock investors. Of special interest is the *S&P Earnings Guide* and the various *Industry Reports*. The *S&P Outlook* recommends stocks, rates them for financial strength, and maintains suggested portfolios based on S&P's stock-rating system. Most of these products are available at libraries. S&P also publishes *Moody's Handbook of Dividend Achievers*. S&P's parent company—McGraw-Hill—publishes *Business Week*, which does ratings on companies and mutual funds on a regular basis.

The Value Line Investment Survey, www.valueline.com, (800) 535-9648, P.O. Box 3988, New York, NY 10008-3988. Although their Web site is truly disappointing given the strength of their investment survey, Value Line is still a primary source of information for stock investors. The investment survey features all of the fundamental data you need to get started. The print product, at $570 a year, is only worthwhile if you are a serious, active stock picker. It's also available on CD-ROM. Value Line also publishes a mutual-fund product.

Publications

Barron's, www.barrons.com. Featuring the best writing and reporting on investments, *Barron's* is a must-read for serious investors. Also covers bonds, mutual funds, real estate, commodities, and dividend news.

Forbes, www.forbes.com. Regularly devotes sections to investing that feature provocative columnists and quarterly mutual-fund reviews.

The Greenmoney Journal, www.greenmoney.com. This bimonthly newsletter is an excellent source on socially responsible investing.

Investor's Business Daily, www.ibd.com. A lightweight version of the *Wall Street Journal, IBD* is full of stock tips.

Kiplinger's Personal Finance, www.kiplingers.com. A general magazine on personal finance and investing, *Kiplinger's* is a good place to start if you don't have much investment experience.

Mutual Funds, www.mutualfunds.com. The sister publication of *Money* magazine, *Mutual Funds* does exactly what you'd think, profiling leading mutual funds. Although the magazine is hot on the best-performing funds, avoid it if you are a long-term investor.

Smart Money, www.smartmoney.com. The most readable magazine on investing and personal finance.

The Wall Street Journal, www.wsj.com. A combination of first-rate reporting and research, the *Journal's* Marketplace section is the place to start for investment trends.

Worth, www.worth.com. A good resource if you have a lot of money and you are focusing on maintaining your lifestyle or giving away your money to worthy causes.

Web Sites

Barra, www.barra.com. A data source for risk and return predictions.

CERES, www.ceres.org. An organization promoting corporate environmental responsibility.

CNN, fn.cnn.com. A fountain of information on investing and markets.

EDGAR, www.edgar-online.com or www.sec.gov. On-line filings of public companies including annual/quarterly reports and proxy statements. Look for "10-ks" to get detailed information on companies. This is the stuff they have to tell the government.

The Fidelity Group, www.fidelity.com. A commercial site for Fidelity's funds, it features some excellent calculators and articles on investing and retirement.

Financeware.com, www.financeware.com. A site featuring portfolio selection software.

Financial Engines, www.financialengines.com. Drawing on the intellectual support of Nobel Laureate William Sharpe, this site provides a risk-adjusted portfolio management system.

Hoovers Business Information, www.hoovers.com. A good source, even for non-members, of basic business information.

Interfaith Center for Corporate Responsibility, www.iccr.org. A group promoting international corporate responsibility.

Kanon, Bloch, Carré, www.kanon.com. Although designed to sell you money management and research services, the site offers excellent background on investment performance.

Multinational Monitor, www.essential.org/monitor. A group that monitors irresponsible corporate behavior across the world.

Money, www.money.com. Having consistently read the magazine for years, I can tell you the Web site is much more useful, featuring calculators and articles galore.

Quicken, www.quicken.com. Although linked to Intuit's popular sofware by the same name, this site continues to amaze me with its bountiful calculators, articles, and tips on investing.

Responsible Wealth, www.responsiblewealth.org. The group promotes the idea that your wealth can make a difference around the world.

Social Investment Forum, www.socialinvest.org. The trade group representing socially responsible investors.

Sustainable Business, www.sustainablebusiness.com. A group that promotes sustainable business practices.

T. Rowe Price, www.troweprice.com. A commercial site featuring excellent planning software for retirement or college financing. They also publish a newsletter for investors.

Thestreet.com, www.thestreet.com. If you are addicted to following the market day to day, this is the site for you.

The Vanguard Group, www.vanguard.com. Although this a commercial site peddling Vanguard's funds, the investor education section has strong articles on mutual funds, retirement, and college saving as well as a mutual-fund cost calculator.

Zacks Investment Research, www.zacks.com. A site dedicated to earnings reports and investment analysis.

Appendix 2:
How to Find Money to Invest

Our journey continues, but this is the last stop, honest. If, for some reason, you made it this far and are still flummoxed about how to save money, then here are a few bits of advice:

1. Forget the budget, just save. Budgets don't work for everyone, so just invest at least 10 percent of your annual income and set aside at least four months' worth of expenses in a money-market account.

2. Save automatically each month. You can set up an automatic withdrawal from your checking account into your money-market fund. Simply give your banking information to your fund manager and they will electronically debit your checking account for a set amount each month. If you can't touch it, you can't spend it.

3. Save for your goals. Planning to buy a new home, car, or appliances? Save for it. Pay cash. Don't put it on your credit card and you'll save on finance charges.

4. Only use your credit card for things you will have the money for. If you pay off your credit card balance each month, you are not spending beyond your means.

5. Fully fund all of your long-term investment accounts. These include 401(k)s, 403(b)s, college-savings plans, Roth IRAs, SEP-IRAs, Keoghs, SIMPLEs, and Education IRAs. Money growing tax-deferred always beats money that you hand over to Uncle Sam. If you have spare cash from a bonus, windfall, or inheritance, tuck away the maximum allowed in tax-deferred accounts.

Index

About the Author

JOHN F. WASIK is a columnist for Bloomberg News, an award-winning editor/writer/speaker/lecturer, and the author of nine books, including *The Late-Start Investor*, *The Kitchen-Table Investor*, and *Retire Early—and Live the Life You Want Now*.

As an investigative reporter, he has been honored with the Donald Robinson Award for Investigative Journalism (ASJA), the National Press Club Consumer Journalism Award, the "Best of the Best" Award for Business Writing (SPJ), the American Society on Aging National Media Award, the Peter Lisagor Award for Consumer Journalism, and the Medill/Strong Award for Financial Journalism.

As an independent writer, his original pieces have appeared in *Reader's Digest*, the *New York Times*, *Parade*, *Better Homes & Gardens*, *Popular Science*, *Barron's*, *The Saturday Evening Post*, *Modern Maturity*, *Mother Jones*, *The Progressive*, *Entrepreneur*, *Marketing News*, the *Chicago Tribune*, and *Health*.